digital photography
handbook

digital photography handbook

mark l. chambers

Hungry Minds™

New York, NY ● Cleveland, OH ■ Indianapolis, IN

Digital Photography Handbook

Published by
Hungry Minds, Inc.
909 Third Avenue
New York, NY 10022
www.hungryminds.com

Library of Congress Control Number: 2001016711

ISBN: 0-7645-3517-X

Printed in the United States of America

10 9 8 7 6 5 4 3 2 1

1B/RY/QU/QR/IN

Distributed in the United States by Hungry Minds, Inc.

Distributed by CDG Books Canada Inc. for Canada; by Transworld Publishers Limited in the United Kingdom; by IDG Norge Books for Norway; by IDG Sweden Books for Sweden; by IDG Books Australia Publishing Corporation Pty. Ltd. for Australia and New Zealand; by TransQuest Publishers Pte Ltd. for Singapore, Malaysia, Thailand, Indonesia, and Hong Kong; by Gotop Information Inc. for Taiwan; by ICG Muse, Inc. for Japan; by Intersoft for South Africa; by Eyrolles for France; by International Thomson Publishing for Germany, Austria, and Switzerland; by Distribuidora Cuspide for Argentina; by LR International for Brazil; by Galileo Libros for Chile; by Ediciones ZETA S.C.R. Ltda. for Peru; by WS Computer Publishing Corporation, Inc., for the Philippines; by Contemporanea de Ediciones for Venezuela; by Express Computer Distributors for the Caribbean and West Indies; by Micronesia Media Distributor, Inc. for Micronesia; by Chips Computadoras S.A. de C.V. for Mexico; by Editorial Norma de Panama S.A. for Panama; by American Bookshops for Finland.

For general information on Hungry Minds' products and services please contact our Customer Care department within the U.S. at 800-762-2974, outside the U.S. at 317-572-3993 or fax 317-572-4002.

For sales inquiries and reseller information, including discounts, premium and bulk quantity sales, and foreign-language translations, please contact our Customer Care department at 800-434-3422, fax 317-572-4002 or write to Hungry Minds, Inc., Attn: Customer Care Department, 10475 Crosspoint Boulevard, Indianapolis, IN 46256.

For information on licensing foreign or domestic rights, please contact our Sub-Rights Customer Care department at 212-884-5000.

For information on using Hungry Minds' products and services in the classroom or for ordering examination copies, please contact our Educational Sales department at 800-434-2086 or fax 317-572-4005.

For press review copies, author interviews, or other publicity information, please contact our Public Relations department at 212-884-5000 or fax 212-884-5400.

For authorization to photocopy items for corporate, personal, or educational use, please contact Copyright Clearance Center, 222 Rosewood Drive, Danvers, MA 01923, or fax 978-750-4470.

 is a trademark of Hungry Minds, Inc.

 HP and the HP logo are registered trademarks of Hewlett-Packard Company

About the Author

Mark L. Chambers has been an author, computer consultant, BBS sysop, programmer, and hardware technician for more than 15 years. His first love affair with a computer peripheral blossomed in 1984, when he bought his high-tech 300 bps modem—now he spends entirely too much time on the Internet. His favorite pastimes include watching Louisiana State University football, collecting gargoyles, playing his three pinball machines, fixing and upgrading computers, playing the latest computer games, and rendering 3D flights of fancy—and during all that, he listens to just about every type of music imaginable.

With degrees in journalism and creative writing from LSU, Mark took the logical career choice and started programming computers. However, after five years as a COBOL programmer for a hospital system, he decided that there must be a better way to earn a living, and he became the documentation manager for a well-known communications software developer. Somewhere in between organizing and writing software manuals, Mark began writing computer books; his first book, *Running a Perfect BBS*, was published in 1994. He now writes full-time, producing several books a year, and provides technical editing for other books his publishers throw at him. You can leave him mail by visiting his Web page at www.geocities.com/SiliconValley/Bay/4373/index.html.

Mark is also the author of *Building a PC For Dummies*, *Scanners For Dummies*, *Hewlett-Packard Official Printer Handbook*, *Hewlett-Packard Official Recordable CD Handbook*, *Recordable CD Bible*, and *Teach Yourself the iMac Visually* (all published by Hungry Minds, Inc., formerly known as IDG Books Worldwide), as well as *Official Netscape Navigator Guide to Web Animation*, *Windows 98 Optimizing*, *Troubleshooting Little Black Book*, and *Running a Perfect BBS*.

Credits

Acquisitions Editor
John Gravener

Project Editor
Laura E. Brown

Technical Editor
Kristen Tod

Copy Editor
Michael D. Welch

Project Coordinator
Joe Shines

Graphics and Production Specialists
Gabriele McCann, Laurie Stevens, Brian Torwelle

Quality Control Technician
Susan Moritz

Book Designer
Michelle Logan

Proofreading and Indexing
York Production Services, Inc.

Cover Image
© Hewlett-Packard Company

To the best in-laws a man could ask for, Frank and Vera Judycki —
or, as their grandchildren call them, Maw-Maw and Paw-Paw.

Foreword

The way we take and share pictures is changing. The era of digital imaging is here, and with it come limitless possibilities. A blending of both creativity and technology, digital imaging enables people to capture and share memories and experiences in the most convenient, versatile, and expressive manner ever.

Digital cameras now exist to suit just about everyone's needs—from the casual user who just wants to take snapshots of family and friends to professionals looking for cameras with the creative controls to support special photographic techniques. As camera resolution improves, storage capacity increases, scanners become easier to use, and software tools to manipulate digital images proliferate, interest in digital imaging will continue to grow.

Digital cameras are a perfect fit with the new digital consumer lifestyle. Images are available instantly. They can be shared over the Internet or beamed to printers wirelessly, and they can be printed as often as desired on specialty paper with today's home inkjet printers. This instant image generation offers a degree of freedom that is simply unobtainable with traditional photographic prints.

This handbook contains everything you need to get started with digital imaging and, when ready, move on to more advanced techniques. Basic photographic skills (such as shot composition, lighting, and exposure) are covered, as are topics specific to digital imaging, such as image editing, electronic file formats, and special crafts projects that you can create with an inkjet printer.

It is with pleasure that I recommend this volume to anyone interested in learning more about digital imaging.

Andrew Tallian
Vice President of Worldwide Marketing
Consumer Business
Hewlett-Packard Company

Preface

About five years ago, I was leafing through my favorite photography magazine, admiring the stunning shots taken by professionals and lusting after the features of cameras that I couldn't afford, when my eye chanced to fall on a particular article. "Digital cameras," this article stated, "are on their way down in price, and eventually they'll actually overtake traditional film cameras in popularity." I distinctly remember chuckling to myself about the idea that an amateur photographer like me would ever want—or need—a digital camera. After all, I already had a 35mm SLR and a scanner that I could use to create digital images from my prints . . . and the technology was so expensive and complex! "No way," I told myself. "Digital cameras will remain toys for professionals, real-estate agents, and the wealthy for a long time to come."

Believe me, I wasn't just *mistaken*—I was *way* off base! Five years later, I'm an avid digital photographer, I own two digital cameras, I'm shopping for a third, and I've switched subscriptions to two well-known digital photography magazines. What I didn't understand then was the sheer convenience of a digital camera, how quickly the prices would drop . . . and just how good the image quality could become. Although a typical automatic digital camera is still significantly more expensive than its "point-and-shoot" film counterpart, it's now as easy to use, and it's actually cheaper to own over the long run. Plus, combine a digital camera with an inkjet printer, and you're ready to create customized crafts, such as greeting cards and T-shirts and even business cards—or perhaps you'd rather use your images on the Web or send them to friends and family through e-mail.

There's a catch, though—if you're shopping for a digital camera or you're just starting out, you'll soon be knee-deep in features that you've probably never heard of (as well as computer acronyms that make no sense at all). Plus, you'll need a basic background in the existing technology of all cameras, whether they save images on disk or film.

I wrote this book with the novice digital photographer in mind, and I think that you'll find it a complete introduction to this exciting hobby—or this powerful business tool. You'll find the information necessary to buy the right camera to fit your needs, to set it up, and to take everything from basic snapshots to more serious works of art.

Who Should Read This Book?

The *Digital Photography Handbook* was designed for any owner of a PC or Macintosh who needs information about today's digital cameras. It's been especially written for readers who are:

- Computer novices or those who have a basic knowledge of personal computers
- Currently shopping for a camera or who have just bought one
- Interested in the technology of digital image capture
- Interested in improving their photographs through composition and editing
- Experiencing problems with installing, configuring, or using a digital camera

It's important to note that this book is not specifically geared toward owners of Hewlett-Packard cameras or printers. Although I do use Hewlett-Packard cameras and printers as examples for step-by-step projects, you'll benefit from the information you'll find here no matter what brand or model of digital camera you're using.

How This Book Is Organized

The chapters are organized into four parts, as follows:

- **Part I, "Getting Started in Digital Photography,"** explains the technology behind both traditional film and digital cameras. I show you how you can determine your needs and select the right camera, and then I show you how to connect it to your computer and prepare it for use.
- **Part II, "General Digital Photography Techniques,"** discusses the details you should know that pertain exclusively to digital cameras: how to transfer, view, print, and store images.
- **Part III, "Advanced Digital Photography Topics,"** moves farther into the realm of the serious photographer, introducing you to lighting, exposure, lenses, composition, image file formats, and image-editing programs.
- **Part IV, "Digital Photography Projects,"** provides tips on taking candid and scenic photographs. It also offers a gallery of great photography from Michael Welch and yours truly as examples of what you can do. Finally, I've provided chapters on the creative side of image editing and a number of fun projects you can try with your images.

I've provided a glossary at the back of the book for your easy reference when tracking down a specific term or acronym, as well as several common digital camera problems and solutions taken from the Hewlett-Packard Technical Support department.

Where to Go from Here

You can take one of three directions through the book:

* If you're considering buying a digital camera or you're interested in the technology behind digital photography, start from Chapter 1.

* If you need help starting out with a brand new digital camera, jump to Chapter 3 and begin reading there. Once you're comfortable with your camera, you can read the earlier chapters of the book at your leisure.

* Finally, if you've owned your digital camera for some time and you'd like to learn more about advanced digital photography, start with Chapter 7 — again, you can read the earlier chapters later.

Acknowledgments

This book is a highly visual piece of work, so I have many people to thank for their help with both the words *and* the images!

First, a round of heart-felt thanks to Michael Welch for his stunning images that you'll find showcased within this book! Michael has traveled the world with his cameras, and his uncanny eye for composition has proven itself in photographs of every genre. I was incredibly lucky to be able to pick images from a selection of his photographs that complemented my work perfectly. You'll find a presentation of his haiku (melded with many of the images here) online at www.family-net.net/~brooksbooks/welch/index.html. (It's fortunate that he also happens to be the copy editor for this book as well!)

Next, it's time to thank my technical editor, Kristen Tod, who helped ensure that "pixels" didn't get mixed up with "f-stops" throughout by balancing knowledge of both film and digital cameras.

This is my *third* title in the Hewlett-Packard Press series — wow, I like typing that!— and I'd like to thank the great folks at HP who assisted me every step of the way. Along with the staff at HP technical support, my special appreciation goes to Pat Pekary, Susan Wright, Stephen Hall, and Tanya Maurer.

I know how much extra work it takes to lay out and produce a full-color masterpiece like this book — and, as always, the fantastic production crew at Hungry Minds, Inc., came through without a scratch. They're the best in the business!

As with every book I've written, I'd like to thank my wife Anne, and my children, Erin, Chelsea, and Rose, for their support and love — and for letting me follow my dream!

Finally, two very hard-working people at Hungry Minds, Inc. deserve *all* of the appreciation that I can shoehorn into a single paragraph of text. My acquisitions editor, John Gravener, gave me a chance to showcase my photography (and deliver another great HP Press title), and I appreciate that he invited me to take on this great project. And my project editor, Laura E. Brown — what can I say? Her untiring dedication to this book kept all of us on an even keel, even with a headache-inducing schedule and a very complex layout jammed with dozens of photographs. My best to both of you — and if you ever need a photographer for weddings and special occasions, you both know where to turn!

Contents at a Glance

Contents

Part IV: Digital Photography Projects   103

digital photography handbook

E-mailing a Family Photo

Everyone has an e-mail address these days — so you can send your digital photographs to just about anyone! It's easy to send your latest candid shots to Aunt Harriet — no printing, envelopes, or expensive postage necessary. As long as you both have an Internet connection and an e-mail account that can receive binary attachments — virtually every e-mail setup can — you're ready to go! With your digital camera, you can snap a series of images and place them in your friend's e-mail Inbox in just a few minutes.

In this QuickStart, we'll take a digital family photograph that you've downloaded to your computer and e-mail it to someone using Microsoft Outlook.

▲ **Tip**

Most Internet Service Providers place a ceiling of anywhere from 2 to 5MB on an e-mail attachment, so it's always a good idea to convert your images to JPEG format before sending them. Luckily, most digital cameras now produce images in this format, so your photographs are probably fine as-is. If you do need to convert your photographs to JPEG format, however, turn to Chapter 10 for all the details on conversion.

Follow these steps to e-mail a family photo:

1. Double-click the Microsoft Outlook icon on your Windows desktop to run Outlook.

2. Choose File ➪ New and then select Mail Message from the pop-up menu. Outlook opens an untitled message window like the one shown in Figure QS.1.

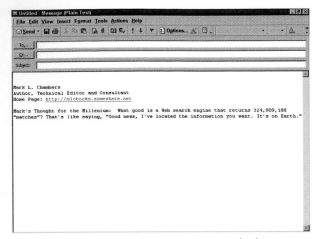

Figure QS.1 Creating a new message in Outlook.

3. Click your cursor in the To field and type an e-mail address, or click the To button and choose an entry from your Address Book.

4. Click in the editing pane and type the text of your message.

5. Now attach the image — choose Insert⇨File from the menu to display the Insert File dialog box shown in Figure QS.2.

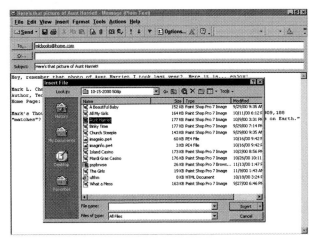

Figure QS.2 Select the image to attach from this dialog box.

6. Navigate to the location where you saved the image and click the file name once to highlight it.

7. Click the arrow next to the Insert button and choose Insert as Attachment from the pop-up menu. Outlook adds an attachment pane to the bottom of the window and displays the attached file icon, as shown in Figure QS.3.

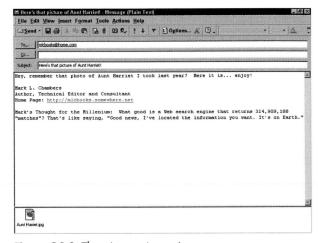

Figure QS.3 There's your image!

8. Finally, click the Send button on the toolbar to send the message.

If the recipient of your message also uses Microsoft Outlook, it's easy for them to save the attachment to disk — right-click the attachment icon and choose Save As from the pop-up menu to display the Save As dialog box shown in Figure QS.4.

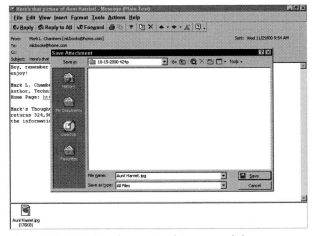

Figure QS.4 Saving the received image to disk.

Getting Started in Digital Photography

The Basics of Digital Photography

IN THIS CHAPTER
- Why try a digital camera?
- How does a digital camera work?
- A quick history of photography
- Moving from film to digital
- Digital photography as a hobby
- Digital photography in the workplace

On the surface, the arrival of the digital camera seems to signal a complete revolution in photography—there's no film, no darkroom and no development, so most folks seem to think that a digital camera looks different, operates differently, and produces different results from a traditional film camera.

Actually, a digital camera is quite similar to a film camera. In fact, I'll be discussing many of the same topics in this book that you'd find in a book about film photography, including lenses, aperture, shutter speed, focal length, and depth of field. (If you're a beginner and these terms sound like ancient Greek, don't worry—I'll cover all of them in detail later.)

So why is digital photography such a big hit these days? Why are more and more photographers making the switch to pictures composed of "bits and bytes" instead of exposed film? To sum it all up in a single word, the answer is *convenience*! With a digital camera, you have freedom that no film camera can match.

This chapter introduces you to digital cameras—including how they work and why they're so popular.

Why Try a Digital Camera?

Today's digital cameras offer convenience and freedom that an old-fashioned film camera just can't equal. But what does that mean? It sounds a little too much like advertising copy, doesn't it? Okay, then, it's time to get down to specifics and talk about precisely what a digital camera can do for you.

They're cheaper to use

First (and foremost for many digital photographers) is the money you'll save with a digital camera—there's no film to buy, and no development necessary for your pictures. If you'll view most of your pictures on your computer's screen or send them to friends and family through Internet e-mail, there's really no extra cost involved besides a few batteries!

Tip
I recommend a good battery charger as well as reusable, rechargeable batteries for any digital photographer — the entire recharging system quickly pays for itself. Check to ensure that your camera supports the use of rechargeable batteries, though, as some low-end cameras do not (such as the HP PhotoSmart 210 and 215 cameras).

If you do print your pictures, however, it's a good idea to use glossy or matte photo paper to achieve the best results from your pictures. Photo paper is significantly more expensive than plain inkjet paper, but with a good inkjet printer you'll get results that are very close to a photograph taken with a typical automatic 35mm film camera—colors look brighter, and a photo will last much longer in your album if printed on photo paper. Photo paper is available in several sizes, including standard 4×6 (snapshot) and 8×10 (enlargement) formats. In many cases your enlargements can cost less to print yourself than going back to the photo processor or lab (for example, \$1.50 versus \$6.00 for an 8×10).

Tip
Before you use one of those expensive sheets of photo paper, print a test page using plain paper to make sure that your image is correctly sized and aligned!

There's no developing time

Why wait several days (or even an hour) to see how your photos turned out? If you have access to your computer, you can download, choose which images you want, and then print your photographs in a few minutes. *Downloading* is a term for transferring files to your computer that dates back to the early days of computer bulletin board systems and modems; however, you don't need a modem to use your camera, because your image files are copied from your camera over a cable connection.

If you want to share your photographs in record time, consider the HP PhotoSmart inkjet printer shown in Figure 1.1—with this hardware, you don't even need to turn on your computer to print your photos! The PhotoSmart printer accepts the same memory card "film" used in today's digital cameras, so you can simply unload your memory card from your camera and plug it directly into your printer.

Figure 1.1 With the HP PhotoSmart inkjet printer, you can print your photos without using your computer.

Cross-Reference

I talk more about this new printer feature in Chapter 5.

Easy editing with your computer

As an experienced photographer (using both film and digital cameras), I know how frustrating it is to snap that perfect candid photo on your vacation — you know, the one of you deep inside the Great Pyramid in Egypt — only to find that your entire family has a bad case of the "red eye" after the film's been developed! With a traditional print, you could possibly have it retouched for a small fortune, but with a photo from a digital camera, *you* can edit that image yourself, on your computer. Heck, you can even remove Uncle Milton, if you like!

Later in the book, I discuss both basic and advanced image editing, and you'll learn how to perform true photographic magic with your mouse: cropping, resizing, mirroring, enhancing, or even adding elements that you could never imagine with a film negative. (That's how I ended up in the picture in Figure 1.2.) Once you've gained experience improving your digital photographs, you'll wonder how you got along without your trusty image editor — and, like me, you'll probably have three or four of these cool programs on your computer.

Ready to print, send, or display

It's a fact — friends and family absolutely crave photographs. With a film camera, the drill is always the same: wait for several sets of your prints, stuff them in envelopes and send them halfway across the country. It costs money, and those pictures will take days to arrive, but what else can you do? Well, with a digital camera and an Internet account, you've licked your last stamp! Here's what you can do:

- Once you've downloaded your images to your computer, they can be enclosed in e-mail messages.

- Do you have family members without Internet access? You can save your images onto floppy disks, or print them on glossy paper (or greeting cards, or even T-shirts).

- Feel like showing off your prized pictures at work? Those images can be displayed on your screen or even made into your desktop background on your PC or Macintosh.

- Need a screen saver? You can create your own custom computer screen saver with your own pictures.

- With a CD recorder, you can even make a slide show on a CD-ROM that will last for decades.

Figure 1.2 It's good to have famous friends, don't you think?

Note

◢ If you don't already have a CD recorder installed on your computer, I can recommend the perfect book on the subject: the *Hewlett-Packard Official Recordable CD Handbook*, written by Mark L. Chambers (yours truly) and published by Hungry Minds, Inc., formerly known as IDG Books Worldwide.

Preview before you save

Ever run out of film in the middle of a wedding reception? With a traditional camera, you're going to find yourself in the car, making a quick run to the nearest convenience store to buy a roll of hideously overpriced film. By the time you're back, the bride and groom are on their way to their honeymoon spot, and the only photo opportunity left is snapping someone sweeping up the rice.

Or consider this situation: You're taking a very important photo of four generations of your family, all gathered for a grand reunion that happens only once every decade. There's no second chance with a typical film camera. Although you can take an entire roll of photos of that gathering, you can't tell what those photographs will look like with a regular 35mm camera. (I'd suggest a visit to your local one-hour development lab, just in case.) No pressure, right?

A digital camera with an LCD screen (which is practically a standard feature these days) solves both of these dilemmas for you:

- **Delete unnecessary images.** If you're running out of space on a memory card — roughly the same situation as running out of film — you can delete one or more images from the memory card to save space. Using the LCD screen, you can preview each image on the memory card, and delete those that you don't need (or those that didn't come out quite as well as you hoped).

- **Make sure you got the shot.** You can review a photograph on the LCD screen as soon as you take it, so you can make sure that everyone in that important reunion photo is looking toward the camera and smiling, and you didn't cut Uncle Milton in half!

Of course, I'll show you how you can review (and delete) images later in the book.

Tip

▲ If you're careful and you always carry additional rolls of film on trips and photo shoots, make sure you buy an additional memory card or two for your digital camera. As with a standard film camera, you can remove a full memory card and insert an empty one in your digital camera in the time-honored tradition. It helps to be prepared, no matter which type of camera you use.

How Does a Digital Camera Work?

"Wait a minute . . . don't get technical on me all of a sudden. Do I *really* need to know how digital cameras work?" Definitely not! As with your computer or your VCR, you don't actually need to know how things work inside to use your digital camera — just skip ahead to the next section. However, if you're interested in how light is captured in bits and bytes, read on and learn what's happening behind the scenes.

First things first

Before I explain the alchemy behind digital images, I should quickly cover how a traditional film camera works; as I said before, the two types of cameras share many similar parts, and they work using the same concepts.

Figure 1.3 illustrates the process of taking a film exposure. Let's follow the process step by step:

1. You remove the lens cap (or, in the case of a typical "point-and-shoot" automatic, you move the protective slide away from the lens, which turns on the camera).

2. As you press the camera's shutter button, the shutter opens for a fraction of a second.

3. Light from the subject passes through the lens and shutter and into the body of the camera. The lens can often be adjusted to bring objects at different distances into clear view; this is called *focusing*.

4. The light strikes the surface of the film, which causes a chemical reaction in the film's silver-halide surface. This process is called *exposure*.

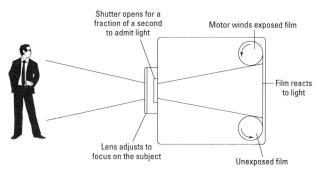

Figure 1.3 The process of taking a film photograph.

5. The motor inside the camera automatically advances the film to the next section, ready to take another photograph — or, if your camera uses manual winding, you turn a wheel or crank to advance the film to the next frame.

Naturally, all these steps take only a second or two, but the shutter is open long enough to record every detail of the scene. When you drop your film off for processing, the development lab develops a negative (or reverse image) from the exposed film, which is then used to create the actual print.

If you remember your science classes, the human eye works along the same lines. Instead of passing through a shutter, however, the light passes through the lens and the iris to focus light onto the *retina* at the back of the eye, which contains millions of light-sensitive nerves that react to color, movement, and shapes. The image is sent through the optic nerve from the eye to your brain. Figure 1.4 illustrates this process.

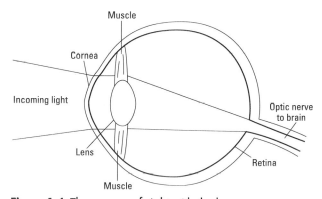

Figure 1.4 The process of sight with the human eye.

Let's go digital!

Now let's move to the same process — capturing an image — using digital technology. As you can see in Figure 1.5, many of the steps are performed exactly the same as with a film camera:

1. You remove the lens cap and turn on the camera — or move the protective slide away from the lens, which turns on the camera automatically.

2. As you press the camera's shutter button, the shutter opens for a fraction of a second.

3. The lens is adjusted to bring the subject into clear view — typically, digital cameras use automatic focusing — and light from the subject passes through the lens and shutter and into the body of the camera.

4. The light strikes the surface of a series of photosensitive sensors (called an *array*) at the back of the camera. Most of today's digital cameras use CCD chips (that's short for "charge-coupled device," if you enjoy the details) as silicon "receptors" for the incoming light. These sensors generate an electrical current when struck by light.

5. The electrical signal from each sensor is processed by the camera's electronics, and the combined "map" of signals is converted into a digital image. Remember, the image doesn't actually exist as a series of patterns that your eye would recognize. Instead, it exists as a series of zeros and ones. These zeros and ones are actually binary data — the universal language used and understood by computers around the world.

6. The completed image is stored in the camera's memory card, which stores it — just like your computer's hard drive stores data.

7. The CCD sensors are "reset" to prepare them for the next image.

As you can see, the digital camera must perform a number of extra steps to take a photograph. When you're shooting photos with a film camera, you can usually take another exposure as soon as the film has advanced, but most digital cameras require a second or two to prepare for the next image.

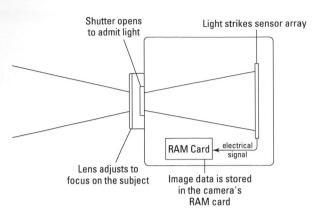

Figure 1.5 The process of taking a digital photograph.

Note

Today's highest-resolution digital cameras don't use a CCD array — they actually have only a single line of sensors, so they're called *linear* CCD cameras. Because a linear CCD camera captures only a single line of the image at a time, it takes several minutes of exposure to finish the photograph — however, these cameras are perfect for taking shots of product boxes, works of art such as sculpture and paintings, and other static subjects. Naturally, these expensive cameras are anything but "point-and-shoot," so I won't be covering them in this book!

A Quick History of Photography

Although the digital camera first appeared on the computer scene in the early 1990s, photography has been a human passion since 1826, when the first crude photographs were taken using a *camera obscura* (that's Latin for "dark chamber") — the same device used by artists and engineers of the time to trace images of buildings and objects. By using a pinhole opening and a series of mirrors, the image from the outside world was reflected on a sheet of glass, where a piece of onionskin paper was placed. All the artist had to do was sketch the outlines. Instead of a sheet of paper, the French inventor Joseph Niepce placed a pewter sheet coated with chemicals on the glass, and voilà — after a whopping eight hours of exposure, he had captured

history's first photograph! Niepce, who lived in the small French town of St-Loup-de-Varennes, called the image a *heliograph* (Greek for "sun writing"). Figure 1.6 illustrates Niepce's camera at work.

Niepce later teamed up with Daguerre, another Frenchman, who advanced the science behind photography by producing a superior copper plate with a silver finish that delivered a clearer and more detailed image — but the subject had to remain still for more than half an hour for a complete exposure. These images were called *daguerreotypes*.

Early cameras built in the last half of the 19th century tended to be unwieldy monsters that only dedicated professionals or fanatical amateurs could handle. Unlike today's cameras, the photographer had to develop the fragile plates (which were made of glass) immediately, and had to cover the back of the camera with a drape of black velvet while exposing the plates to light. As you can imagine, this was hardly a fun process — it was expensive, time-consuming, and very delicate work.

In 1895, George Eastman changed all that. His Kodak company introduced the inexpensive Pocket Kodak camera, which used a film roll instead of a photographic plate, and true amateur photography was born. Instead of developing glass plates, the camera owner simply sent the roll of film back to Kodak for development. The Brownie — introduced in 1900 — was inexpensively priced at $1.00, and more than 100,000 of them were sold in the first year they were on the market! (It's no coincidence that the convenience of these first Kodak cameras was the key to their success, just like the digital cameras we're discussing now.)

As time passed, cameras were improved with the addition of shutters and lenses that could be focused, and the size of the camera body shrunk to a manageable size. Better film was developed that

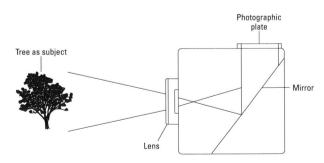

Figure 1.6 Photography using a camera obscura.

could capture motion at faster speeds without blurring. The addition of an automatic winding mechanism made the camera even easier to use.

Today's film cameras range from the simplest and cheapest disposable cameras (where the photographer actually turns in the entire "single-use" camera for development) to the sophisticated 35mm cameras used by professional sports and portrait photographers. Although most photographers prefer color film, many hobbyists like to experiment with black-and-white and infrared film for artistic shots.

Moving from Film to Digital

"So what do I need to do to make the move from film to digital?" That's an easy one: not too much! Besides buying a digital camera (covered in the next chapter), here's a quick checklist:

- **Clean out that darkroom.** If you have darkroom equipment (and you're going to completely switch to digital photography), you can sell all those expensive trays, chemicals, timers, and such on eBay. As a digital photographer, your computer is your darkroom! You can even use your new digital camera to take pictures of your old stuff to post on eBay to increase its appeal.

- **Invest in a good printer.** For the best-looking prints, you'll need an inkjet printer that can deliver photo quality.

- **Tune up your computer.** To make things easier while editing or viewing your images, your computer should have a video card and monitor capable of displaying 16 million colors at resolutions of at least $1,024 \times 768$ or above. Also, I'd recommend that you set aside at least one gigabyte of free hard drive space to store your images before you print them or save them to CD-ROM and have at least 16 to 32MB of RAM.

- **Add a CD recorder.** Take it from someone who's been using digital cameras for many years — get a CD-RW drive (short for "Compact Disc — Rewritable"). You'll find that CD-ROM storage is the most convenient, safe, and permanent method of archiving your digital photographs.

(Plus, you can record your own audio CDs and data CDs, too.)

Most of the other paraphernalia that surrounds film photography will also work with your digital camera, including tripods, lights, meters, camera bags — even that trusty lens cloth! Also, if you have any books on photography, you'll be happy to hear that virtually all the same rules apply when composing or taking a photo (whether you use a digital or film camera).

Digital Photography as a Hobby

For most of this book, I'll be discussing how you can take photographs typically shot by hobbyists — for example, scenic and sports shots, family portraits, and the like. The digital camera is a perfect companion for a hobbyist for a number of reasons:

- **It's easy to experiment.** With a traditional film camera, exercising your creative side takes time — for example, you'll have to wait until that roll of film is processed before you can see precisely how a shot turned out from a certain angle. With a digital camera, you can see the results within seconds, and you can immediately modify your composition to correct errors or add interest to the scene.

- **There's no cost.** As long as you already have your camera, memory cards, your computer, and a good photo-quality printer, you literally have everything you need to explore digital photography — no expensive darkroom equipment or chemicals, no expensive high-resolution film required.

- **Digital cameras are easy to use.** As with film cameras, today's digital cameras offer a wide range of features and functions — including the traditional "point-and-shoot" automatic camera! If you're more interested in simplicity and fun than fancy effects and features, some digital cameras make photography as simple as pressing a single button.

■ **Digital images are great for crafts.** As I mentioned earlier, taking a digital photograph is only half the fun! Naturally, you can print that image on glossy photo paper, but why stop there? You can also create your own greeting cards, T-shirts, stickers, CD and address labels, business cards — even a wine bottle label or two — using your digital image, an inkjet printer, and a printing software suite such as PrintMaster or Print Artist.

▲ Tip

For complete step-by-step instructions on how to create a variety of crafts with your inkjet printer, pick up a copy of the *Hewlett-Packard Printer Handbook*, written by Mark L. Chambers and published by Hungry Minds, Inc., formerly known as IDG Books Worldwide. Also check out Chapter 15, which reviews the same topic.

Digital Photography in the Workplace

The convenience and low cost of a digital camera are also making it a smart choice for businesses of all sizes. For example, because there's no need for development and no cost for film, you can take a photo of each new employee for those ID badges that everyone has to wear without spending half your budget. The photos can probably be downloaded directly to your badge-making program. (No wonder that my new driver's license picture was taken with a digital camera!) Those same images can be used on the company's Web site, too.

Although taking employee pictures is probably the most common use of a digital camera in the workplace, there may be other roles it can play in your business:

■ **Real estate photographs.** With the growing importance of the Web to real-estate agents, they can really benefit from a digital camera — it will save a bundle of money over a few years, and the property pictures can be viewed to make sure they're perfect before to the agent visits the next home. Instead of manually scanning a briefcase full of film prints, property

images taken with a digital camera can be on the company's Web site in just a few minutes.

■ **Product photographs.** Do you need images of your company's products for brochures, press releases, or your online store? Investing in a high-resolution digital camera ensures that you can take those photographs in-house.

■ **Presentations.** Need a quick snapshot of your office or building to personalize a multimedia PowerPoint presentation? With a digital camera, you're no longer forced to use a stock photograph just because there's not enough time to develop and scan a roll of film.

■ **Insurance photographs.** Every insurance agent needs a digital camera for quick snapshots at an accident site. For the same reason, digital cameras are very popular with police and fire investigators.

▲ Tip

It's a good idea for homeowners to keep a record of their belongings for insurance purposes — and the digital camera makes it easy to take a photo or two of every room in your house to record what you own. Once you've collected a complete record of images, record them permanently on a CD-ROM and store the disc in a safety deposit box or other offsite location. Naturally, this won't record serial numbers from your appliances, stereo equipment, and computer system, but it's a simple step you can take once a year that doesn't involve hours of tedious typing. If your digital camera also records audio and attaches it to the picture, you can record additional information about your valuables such as the serial number, approximate worth, size, and so on.

Summary

This chapter opened the door to digital photography — you learned why it's so popular, how digital cameras work in general, and how cameras have developed over the years (pun intended). I also discussed what you'll need to make the change from film to digital, and how the convenience of digital photography appeals to both the hobbyist and the business professional.

Coming up in the next chapter is an overview and recommendations for buying a digital camera.

Buying a Digital Camera

One of my friends who's crazy about his digital camera tells me that it's actually much harder to *buy* the right camera than it is to *use* it! I have to agree. Digital cameras are surrounded by more confusing terms and "must-have" features than just about any other piece of computer hardware. There's certainly more to remember when you're shopping for a digital camera than a comparable film camera.

Many people believe that a digital camera is very different from a traditional film camera. In reality, they are very similar — the big difference is how the image information is recorded: File cameras record the image in an analog format, while digital cameras record information digitally as binary data.

Before we go any farther, let me identify the similarities between the two types of cameras. If you're already familiar with how a film camera works, you'll recognize these terms. If not, don't worry, I explain each of them to you throughout the book. Both types of cameras share the following:

- A light-tight enclosure — the camera body

- A mechanism for focusing light rays onto the film — the lens

- A method of controlling how much light reaches the film — the aperture

- A method for controlling how long the film is exposed to the light — the shutter

- A method for the photographer to see what will be recorded — the viewfinder

- A device for collecting light energy — the sensor

- A method to store the captured images — film, or a memory card

Plus, it's easy to "outgrow" a camera after your first few weeks as a digital photographer. Suddenly, you can find yourself wishing for higher resolution, a larger memory card or a high-speed USB or IEEE-1394/FireWire connection between your camera and your computer. If you simply buy the cheapest camera at your local computer store — or even a brand name that you recognize — you may be disappointed with the results, and in a month or two replace that camera with the one you should have bought. (I know this from experience, as my first digital camera purchase was a disaster!)

In this chapter, I help you avoid these purchasing pitfalls. We begin by evaluating your needs, and then I cover each of the features you should consider when buying your digital camera.

Be Your Own Salesperson!

"Wouldn't it be easier if I just went to the store and talked with a salesperson?" Certainly, that is the traditional process, and there's nothing wrong with asking a salesperson's opinion about digital cameras. To be honest, however, I think that you can do a better job! Here's why:

- **A salesperson has a vested interest in selling you a camera.** Naturally, I'm not saying that a salesperson would steer you in the wrong direction just to make a sale, but you might end up looking at only a handful of brands, and perhaps selecting a camera from only one or two possible choices among those brands. Personally, I'm a big fan of freedom of choice in just about everything, so I would rather make my own selection (usually online, where I can find just about every digital camera made).

- **Not all salespeople know digital cameras.** If you buy your digital camera at a photography store, you're practically certain to find a salesperson who's knowledgeable about the features I discuss in this chapter. And (if my experience is any yardstick) you're also going to pay top dollar for the camera you choose. On the other hand, if you visit a discount store you'll probably get a better price, but it's not likely that you'll encounter a salesperson who's well-acquainted with digital cameras.

- **You may be buying your digital camera online.** With the growing popularity of online shopping, salespeople are becoming a little anachronistic! As an online shopper, you can do all of your research and price comparisons on the Web and pay less than shopping at a local store.

Tip

Are you considering one or two specific digital cameras? Don't forget to take advantage of the product evaluations and reviews you'll find in print and on the Web — unlike most computer hardware, you can also turn to photography magazines as a shopping resource! Try *Digital Camera* magazine (www.photopoint.com/dcm) and *PC Photo* magazine (www.pcphotomag.com).

This chapter leads you through the same process that should be followed by the salesperson at your favorite electronics store: evaluating your needs and discussing the features that you can use for comparison shopping.

What Features Do I Need?

First, determine what type of camera you need — and don't forget, that camera should not only meet your present needs, but offer the additional features you'll grow to appreciate as you begin to take more digital photographs.

For this book, I'll identify three different beginning digital photographers, each of whom needs a different set of features:

■ **The Candid Snapshooter.** Sounds something like a species of exotic bird, doesn't it? Our

Candid Snapshooter demands simplicity and low cost, with a minimum of hassle — this person probably owns a "point-and-shoot" film camera already and is looking for an easy way to create images to send in e-mail or add to a Web page. The Hewlett-Packard PhotoSmart C200 digital camera shown in Figure 2.1 would be just right for most of the folks in this category; it's inexpensive, it holds 40 photos using the default image settings, and it features a typical LCD display that you can use to view your shots after you take them.

■ **The Amateur on a Budget.** The amateur digital photographer expects more from a camera — higher resolution, a faster interface, more memory, and more manual controls. This category usually includes both hobbyists and those people who'll use the camera for business applications such as photographs for reports, presentations, and product Web sites (such as those I discussed in Chapter 1). You're willing to pay more for your camera, but you don't need all the bells and whistles and you'd like to keep the cost down below $300 to $500. As an example camera for this category, the Hewlett-Packard PhotoSmart 315 camera shown in Figure 2.2 offers twice the resolution and more memory than the PhotoSmart C200, plus it uses a faster USB connection.

Figure 2.1 The HP PhotoSmart C200 digital camera — an example of a typical "point-and-shoot" automatic digital camera

Figure 2.2 The HP PhotoSmart 315 digital camera is a typical choice for amateur photographers looking for higher-quality images.

■ **The Professional in Training.** If you're new to digital photography and you fit into this category, you're already a dedicated photographer — either a professional or an experienced amateur — and you're ready to make the leap to digital. Cost is less important than the quality of your equipment and the complete control you can exercise over your images. A typical camera in this category starts at a minimum of $800. You expect all the features that you use on your film camera (such as metering, exposure control, and selectable flash), and you need both a fast shutter speed and a fast downloading rate. The Hewlett-Packard PhotoSmart 912 shown in Figure 2.3 provides high-end features such as manual metering, shutter control, and a 3× optical zoom.

As I discuss each feature in the coming sections, I'll refer back to these categories.

Camera sensors

I mentioned a little about the camera sensor in Chapter 1, but because they are such an important part of your digital camera, you should consider what's available when you're shopping. Although the CCD sensor (charge-couple device) that I mentioned in the first chapter is much more common

because of its high resolution, CMOS sensors consume far less power and support additional image-enhancement features — you'll likely see a large number of CMOS-based cameras within the next few years.

The size of your camera's sensor is important — today's cameras use CCD sensors that measure half an inch (12mm) diagonally; sensors measuring a third and two-thirds of an inch are also available. The larger the sensor, the better because the size of the sensor usually determines the resolution, and (depending on the design) can also improve low-light operation. For example, professional cameras have larger CCD sensors (two-thirds of an inch diagonally), which provide better pictures at low light levels and better enlargements.

Low, medium, and high resolution

It's time to talk pixels! Have you ever noticed how a photograph in a newspaper is actually composed of dots? A *pixel* is a single tiny dot in a digital photograph — your eye combines these individual dots to create the image. (In fact, the same optical quirk of the human eye is used by your computer monitor to display the video information from your programs.) A sensor is made up of an array of receptors, each of which is sensitive to light energy — transforming it into electrical energy.

This similarity between a digital camera and a computer monitor relates to their *resolution*. The resolution of a digital camera (or computer monitor) is commonly listed as the number of pixels that make up the image, measured in rows (left to right) and columns (up and down). For example, a digital image produced with a camera that has a resolution of 640 × 480 means that the image measures 640 pixels horizontally across and 480 pixels vertically.

It's actually pretty easy to gauge the importance of resolution. Here's the general rule: *The higher the numbers, the better the detail delivered by your camera and the better your final image will be.* Every rule has its exceptions, however, as you'll see in cameras that use HP's Imaging Technology, which I discuss in the next section.

Figure 2.3 The HP PhotoSmart 912 is a good example of a high-end digital camera for the professional-in-training.

But I Can Explain!

I'd like to make what I call a "technical confession" (at least I'm being truthful with you). The term *resolution* is bandied about quite a bit in the computer world, and different meanings have appeared for different types of hardware — the result is a difference between the strict definition and the figures you're likely to find when you're researching camera specifications. The original meaning of the term *resolution* applies to the number of pixels per inch in an image, usually expressed as DPI (or *dots per inch*) and PPI (or *pixels per inch*). However, the popular use of the term has slowly come to mean the physical number of pixels in the entire image, as already mentioned.

So why use the term *resolution* when I actually mean the dimension of the image measured in pixels? Well, when you read a typical advertisement or specification sheet for a digital camera that mentions a resolution of 1,024 × 768, they're quoting the actual dimensions of the image in pixels. However, this usage of the term *resolution* is so common — you'll encounter it not only when shopping for a camera, but when discussing monitors and image editors as well — that I'd rather use the same yardstick that just about everyone uses.

For now, here are resolution figures that you're likely to see for today's digital cameras:

- **Low Resolution: 640 × 480/800 × 600.** These cameras produce images suitable for a typical Web page, but they're really not good enough for printed media or business use (especially 640 × 480, which looks quite "jaggy" around the edges when viewed on today's computers or printed on an inkjet printer). If you're a Candid Snapshooter and you find one of these on an online auction (or you scavenge one from a garage sale), they could be a good buy. However, don't expect the high-resolution image quality you'll find in more expensive models.

- **Medium Resolution: 1,152 × 872/1,600 × 1,200.** These are the more common resolutions available today, and they're suitable for an Amateur on a Budget — images look much better when printed, and the detail level is much better than an inexpensive low-resolution camera.

- **High Resolution: 2,000 × 1,312/2,048 × 1,536.** The highest resolutions on the market offer the same level of picture quality you'll find in a true 35mm photograph taken with a film camera, so they're suitable for professional-level work such as for portraits and magazines.

Note that the camera you're evaluating might offer a slightly different resolution (for example, 1,280 × 960), but you should be able to fit it into one of the resolution ranges I've listed. Also, some cameras offer multiple resolutions — you can pack many more images into the same amount of memory by shooting photos at a lower resolution setting, especially if you use compression (which I'll cover later in the chapter).

I should also explain the term *megapixel*, because the more you research digital cameras, the more you'll encounter it. A megapixel is the number of pixels a digital camera's CCD sensor can capture. One megapixel is one million pixels, and two megapixels is two million pixels — you get the idea. Many manufacturers list their cameras with decimals afterwards, as in 1.3 megapixels (approximately 1,300,000 pixels). Most of the cameras currently on the market these days in the $300 range are capable of producing one-megapixel images, while more expensive models deliver two or even three megapixels. The general rule holds true: *the higher the megapixel value, the better final image a digital camera can produce.*

Tip

Are you used to scanning photographs? If so, you're probably aware that the higher the resolution, the more hard drive space a scanner typically needs to store the digital image. Luckily, you won't have that problem with most digital cameras, which store photographs using the very efficient compressed JPEG image format. (More on image formats and compression later in this chapter.) A typical megapixel camera needs only about 200K to store an image.

Introducing HP Imaging Technology

Although most people often see high resolution as the most important feature of a digital camera, you can look for other features in mid-range and high-end cameras that can help improve the image quality of every photograph you take. For example, the HP PhotoSmart 600 and 900 series of digital cameras (and many Pentax digital cameras as well) include HP Imaging Technology, which actually adjusts each shot automatically. These adjustments affect a number of the characteristics of a typical digital image, the most important of which are as follows:

- **Lighting.** HP Imaging Technology adjusts each image for the best appearance under a range of different lighting conditions. (I get into lighting in more detail in Chapter 7.)

- **Color.** Cameras with HP Imaging Technology produce vivid, natural colors and correct skin tones with advanced color balancing (more on this in Chapter 7).

- **Detail.** HP Imaging Technology preserves the detail in both highlights and shadows, producing clearer, sharper images than older digital cameras (and in many cases, even better than film cameras).

To give you some idea of the complex mathematics performed by these HP cameras, they're equipped with an powerful ASIC image processor to accelerate the required calculations after you snap a photograph—this processor can perform over 500 million operations per second, which is comparable to the speed of the early Cray supercomputers!

Of course, I won't go into the technical details of what's going on inside a camera equipped with HP Imaging Technology. Unless you're an engineer or a mathematician (which I'm not), an explanation would likely look like a recipe in a foreign language. However, I can sum up the three advances that make the difference:

- **HP Image Demosaicing.** Although it's a tongue-twister to say and hard to spell, this mathematical algorithm helps fine-tune both the colors and the detail in an image, producing sharp, detailed photographs from sensors with fewer pixels and less distortion (this translates into a less expensive camera, too).

- **Perpetually Accurate Color Balancing.** With this new development, colors in the picture look like what you saw, regardless of the environment. Whether your subject is lit by full sun, overcast, open shade, several types of fluorescent light,

tungsten light, or even a sunset, the colors remain accurate—meaning that you can send most shots directly to your printer, without requiring any adjustments with your computer.

- **Preferred Photographic Reproduction.** A camera with HP Imaging Technology uses PPR to optimize the image for the best possible appearance, much like the adjustments performed by an experienced technician in a professional photo lab. Consider PPR as a "custom photo lab in the camera."

Although HP Imaging Technology still can't guarantee you a perfect shot every time—for example there's no replacement for composition, which I cover in Chapter 9—it can help reduce the problems that most digital photographers encounter in difficult lighting situations.

Camera size and weight

You may not think about the size and body design of your digital camera when you're shopping, but take my word for it: once you've trudged all the way across a huge theme park with a toddler in tow, a few ounces and a few inches can really make a difference! You'll find that virtually all digital cameras fall into these three categories:

- **Point-and-shoot.** This is the digital equivalent of an inexpensive, fully-automatic 35mm camera. A camera of this body style is only about five or six inches long and four inches high, so it fits in a pocket or purse. It's also lightweight, with most point-and-shoot cameras weighing in from 10 to 12 ounces. As you might expect, this is the most popular body style on the market today.

- **Flat body.** A flat-body camera is designed to take advantage of the LCD screen as both a picture preview feature and a "digital" viewfinder—the flat area enables the largest LCD screen possible. (In fact, these cameras may actually lack an old-fashioned optical viewfinder.) These cameras are typically about the size of a paperback book, and they may feature a rotating or swiveling lens system. They're generally in the same weight range as a point-and-shoot camera.

■ **Digital SLR.** If you already own a film single-lens reflex camera (SLR), you're familiar with this body style — when most folks think of a "real" 35mm camera body that uses interchangeable lenses, they're thinking of an SLR body. Digital SLR cameras can be pricey but are very powerful, and they're also large and tend to be heavy compared to a simple point-and-shoot digital camera.

▲ **Tip**

If your DV (short for "digital video") camera can capture still images, it can also do double-duty as a still image digital camera. Keep this in mind while shopping, but remember that these models are primarily designed with video in mind, so they generally don't offer all the features or still image quality of a dedicated still image camera.

So which body type is right for you? Naturally, I recommend the point-and-shoot for most novice photographers, but you can find many choices!

Lenses

Ah, lenses . . . what would a camera be without them? If you're a serious hobbyist or professional, interchangeable lenses are practically a requirement for your camera — if you're a Candid Snapshooter, however, you probably don't want (or need) the hassle of carrying and swapping different lenses. You'll find that digital cameras fall into three categories here as well:

■ **Fixed focus.** Again, we're talking point-and-shoot here. This lens system can capture anything from a foot or two away to the horizon, but you can't manually focus the image, and you typically can't add filters or external lenses. A fixed-focus lens is standard issue on most cameras under $300 or so, and it's all a Candid Snapshooter will ever need. Remember, though, that these cameras wil produce a blurry image if you try to shoot a subject closer than the lens allows.

■ **Auto focus.** If your digital camera has an auto focus feature, it automatically calculates the distance between the lens and the primary subject of your photo and adjusts the focus accordingly. This focusing system is far superior to a fixed

focus system, but it does have its drawbacks: specifically, it takes a second or two for your camera to judge the distance and focus the lens, which means a noticeable pause before the picture is actually taken. Plus, auto focus cameras generally don't do a very good job when shooting through windows, bars, fences, or other obstructions, because they tend to focus for the obstruction and not the subject.

■ **Manual focus.** Professionals and hobbyists alike swear by manual focusing, because it enables you to try artistic effects such as "soft focus" (where the focus is slightly off on purpose). You can also force the camera to focus at a specific distance, which is great for close-up work where the subject is less than a foot away. On the downside, cameras with manual focus control typically cost more than a fixed-focus camera, and you must manually set the focus for each shot (which takes time and practice).

▲ **Tip**

If you'd rather spend less for a camera that doesn't have manual focusing, don't despair — today's image-editing programs can achieve some of the same effects with a click of the mouse!

Some cameras offer a combination of auto focus with manual override control, which includes the best of both worlds — you can snap a quick candid shot, but you can also disable the automatic focus and exercise your creative side with a manual setting.

Finally, we should also consider those cameras that can accept external filters and lenses. If you know you'll be shooting extreme close-ups, wide-angle panoramic scenes, or far-away subjects with a telephoto lens (such as nature photos), your camera should be threaded for a standard lens adapter or be able to use a custom adapter that accepts filters and specialty lenses. Remember, you can't use an image editor to transform a simple snapshot into a panoramic scene!

Zoom

Now that you're an old hand when it comes to focal length, let's change it. If your digital camera has an *optical* zoom feature, it can vary the focal length between lens and sensor array. As the focal length

Let's Talk Focal!

While on the topic of lenses, I need to introduce yet another camera term. This time, it's *focal length*, which is the number of millimeters between the surface of the camera lens and the sensor array in the camera (the one I told you about in Chapter 1). So why do you need to know this trivia? The focal length of your camera determines how large the subject appears in the image — think zoom, which is the next feature I discuss. However, a fixed-focus camera may not have a zoom feature, so you need to shop for a camera with the right focal length in the first place. This figure is easy to remember: a focal length between 35 and 37mm (which offers a slightly wider view) is the industry standard, so if your point-and-shoot digital camera fits in this range, you should be fine.

increases, the subject draws nearer and fills more of the image. On a digital camera, an optical zoom lens works the same as it does on a traditional film camera. You'll generally find one or more levels of optical zoom on medium to higher-priced digital cameras, and everyone (even the Candid Snapshooter) will enjoy this feature. It's worth the cash.

On the other hand, even the most inexpensive cameras usually offer a *digital* zoom, which (for you Monty Python fans) is "something completely different!" With a digital zoom, the focal length on the lens doesn't actually change; instead, the camera's onboard electronics actually enlarges the subject in the existing image to fill more of the frame. Unfortunately, because the number of pixels actually stays the same, the resolution decreases and the picture loses quality when you use digital zoom. Still, digital zoom is a neat feature when you can't get any closer to a subject and you want it larger in the final photograph, and you don't need to resize the image after you've downloaded it to your computer.

Cross-Reference

Chapter 8 includes two figures that help show the difference between optical and digital zoom — for now, just remember that optical is better, but more expensive.

Batteries

And oh, friends and neighbors, do these wonderful toys eat electricity! No matter how much you spend on your digital camera, without the right batteries you'll be stuck with a very high-tech paperweight.

Due to the safety problems involved and the bulk it would add, a digital camera doesn't come with an internal battery charger, such as what a cell phone might use. Let me make an important recommendation: If you're considering a digital camera that uses regular batteries, look for one that accepts rechargeable batteries and buy the rechargeable batteries and a charger if they're not included. If I used regular alkaline batteries in my two digital cameras, I'd end up spending five or six dollars a week just to keep everything going — with my rechargeable system, it costs me only a few pennies instead. Not all digital cameras can use rechargeable batteries, however, so check the camera's manual before using them.

Tip

I recommend using rechargeable batteries and a charger, but I know at times most of us will be forced to use regular batteries in our cameras — and for those occasions, it's important to buy high-drain alkaline or photo lithium batteries. These batteries can provide the extended power that a digital camera needs.

When shopping for a digital camera battery, ask these two questions:

- **Can the camera use rechargeable batteries, and if so, what type?** NiCad rechargeable batteries aren't very effective for high-drain electronic devices, but NiMH (nickel metal hydride) rechargeables work well and come in the common AA size. The best (and most expensive) type is the lithium-ion (usually abbreviated as LIon) rechargeable battery. LIon batteries come in specific sizes for camera brands that accept them — you cannot insert them into a camera in place of AA-sized alkaline batteries unless your camera has an adapter for them, as does the HP PhotoSmart 912. Some cameras include the batteries and a charger as a complete package.

- **What's the camera's average battery life?** Pretty self-explanatory, but you'd be surprised at the difference between different types of cameras. The more expensive models tend to have a larger number of power-hungry features such as large LCD screens and bigger flash units, so they often drain batteries faster. Look for the camera's power consumption rating (and recharge cycle time, if applicable) in its specifications. Look for a camera that has an optical viewfinder in addition to an LCD to save battery life. A color LCD is the largest power drain in a camera — use it sparingly and carry backup batteries.

▲ Tip

If the camera you're considering has a recharger, remember that lithium-ion holds a charge longer and delivers more power than nickel metal hydride (or NiMH) batteries.

Again, a spare set of batteries is a great idea — stick them in your camera case for emergencies, and don't let them go stale.

Flash

To the photography novice, a flash is something that often doesn't go off, and when it does it invariably adds "red-eye." (Don't worry, I'll show you how to get rid of that in Chapter 11.) To a serious amateur or professional photographer, however, a flash unit is a very important piece of equipment, and it should offer as much manual control as possible (along with automatic operation, naturally).

You'll find three types of flash units on today's digital cameras. (Isn't it weird how most of these features appear in threes?) They are:

■ **Automatic.** Standard equipment on most point-and-shoot cameras, and they operate exactly like their counterparts on film cameras. There's no manual control, but I've found that automatic flash usually produces a good exposure for the typical snapshot. Make sure you stay within your camera's flash range. If you are too close, your image can be overexposed (too light). If you're too far away, your image will be underexposed (too dark).

■ **Semi-automatic.** Besides full automatic operation, a semi-automatic flash unit can be set

"always on" or "always off" — for example, you may want to override your automatic flash when shooting a birthday celebration in low light so that you can capture the candles from the cake illuminating the faces around it. This is also a good idea for locations where flash photography is not allowed, such as concert halls, churches, or museums.

■ **Full manual.** Definitely top-of-the-line, and the best choice for the professional sports or portrait photographer. Besides the automatic and semi-automatic capabilities I just described, a full manual flash can be synchronized with external flash units (so it has the required connectors), and the amount of light can be varied to match the lighting needs of a particular environment. You'll usually find a full manual flash only on two-megapixel cameras or greater. Some of these high-end cameras also have a "hot-shoe" adapter to attach an external flash unit.

Some of the most stunning photographs I've ever seen have used light and shadow as creative elements — I strongly recommend that you consider at least a semi-automatic flash unit if you plan on devoting a lot of time to photography as a hobby. When you consider that you can view the results of a photo as soon as you've taken it with a digital camera, it becomes very easy to experiment with a particular flash setting to achieve exactly the effect you're looking for — and later, of course, you can tell everyone that you got it right the very first time!

Image storage

As you learned in Chapter 1, a digital camera stores the images you take as a huge collection of ones and zeroes (called *bits*, the language of computers) until you download them from your camera to your computer or your printer. However, just how those bits get stored varies from camera to camera. It's time to consider what types of image storage you can choose from (*five* options this time):

■ **Memory cards.** The storage solution of choice for most digital cameras, memory cards come in two varieties: CompactFlash and SmartMedia cards, both of which are about half the size of a business card. These function basically the same as the RAM in your computer, but they do not lose information when the camera is turned off, or when they're removed from the camera. You can "format" a memory card to erase the images it holds and reclaim that room. memory cards come in various sizes, so make sure you compare the amount of RAM you're buying when doing your comparison shopping.

- **Memory sticks.** A specialized type of memory card used with a few cameras — as the name suggests, these cards are shaped like a stick of gum.

- **Floppy disks.** No, you read that right. I actually wrote "floppy disks" — did you think they were dead? As a matter of fact, they are for just about all computer users, but some digital cameras can use them for storing images! Naturally, a 1.44MB floppy can't hold as much as an 8MB memory card, but floppies are cheap. If you carry one of these cameras, you can simply eject the floppy disk and load a new one if you run out of room. A single floppy can usually only hold ten (or even fewer) high-resolution images.

- **Hard drives.** Some of today's cameras can also take advantage of miniature hard drives that can store anywhere from 40 to 120MB of images — however, you probably won't find one of these cameras for under $1,000. Naturally, a hard drive can hold more than a typical memory card.

- **PCMCIA cards.** Finally, some of the high-end cameras on the market can use the same PCMCIA cards used in laptops — and because you can remove the card and plug it directly into your laptop, there's no downloading required! One of these cameras can save you a significant amount of time you would otherwise spend waiting in front of your computer.

Formats and compression

More definitions? We can't get away from them! First, an image *format* is the standard data structure that your camera uses to save a photograph; better-known image formats that you may have encountered in your computer and Web travels include BMP (Windows bitmap), TIFF (Tagged Image File Format), GIF (Graphics Interchange Format), and

JPG/JPEG (Joint Photographic Experts Group). The format that your camera uses to save images is important for two reasons:

- **Some formats are space hogs.** Some image formats such as BMP can use an incredible amount of space to store a photograph, making them impractical for use in the limited elbow room provided by a memory card. For this reason, virtually all cameras use JPEG or GIF format to store images. Your camera should definitely use *at least one* of these two formats. For example, a typical megapixel image takes up only about 120K in JPEG format.

Note

Don't discount BMP and TIFF formats completely, however. They provide the best possible image quality, which is why some high-end professional cameras offer these additional formats. They also have built-in hard drives or large-capacity memory cards to store the large files. For example, the HP PhotoSmart 912 digital camera can capture and store image files in either JPEG or uncompressed TIF formats.

- **Popular formats don't need conversion.** I'll be talking more about converting image formats in Chapter 10 — for now, just remember that conversion is something you want to avoid if possible. Because JPEG and GIF file formats are already commonly used on the Web, you won't need to convert them to another image format once you've downloaded your photographs from the camera to your computer. Again, this is another reason why JPEG and GIF are so popular with today's cameras.

Compression is also a space-saving feature on a digital camera — with compression, the size of an image is reduced by actually eliminating some of the pixels using complex mathematical algorithms. (In fact, the JPEG image format that I mentioned earlier contains a built-in compression scheme that your digital camera can use.) With 10 to 20 percent of compression, it's very hard for anyone to tell the difference in the image, so most cameras compress images at this level by default; however, as you increase the compression rate to shrink the file even further, the image quality is significantly degraded as the file size is reduced.

Take my word for it, compression is something that you want to control — and thankfully, most cameras that deliver one megapixel or more offer you at least two or three levels of compression that you can set yourself. They may assign these levels of compression with actual percentages such as 20%/50%/75% (the higher the compression, the more space you save on the memory card and the poorer the image quality), or they may indicate them by rating picture quality as "standard," "fine," and "best" (the better the picture quality, the lower the compression rating and the fewer images you can fit on your memory card). For instance, the HP PhotoSmart C200 camera uses "basic," "fine," and "superfine" quality settings. Check the specifications for any camera you're evaluating for the compression levels it offers.

LCD screens and viewfinders

Virtually all of the least expensive digital cameras on the market these days — by "inexpensive" I mean models that sell for less than $100, for example — offer only an optical viewfinder, which is the viewfinder used on most "point-and-click" film cameras on the market.

I strongly suggest, however, that you buy a digital camera with an LCD screen that can function as a "digital" viewfinder. Personally, I like the "what you see is what you get" functionality of an LCD viewfinder, because you're actually seeing a smaller representation of the final image — it's easier to frame the shot. Also, the LCD screen can display a settings menu, making it much easier to configure your camera's functions. Finally, most cameras with LCD screens include at least some level of image management (which I'll get into later in this chapter), enabling you to delete unwanted images so you can save that valuable space on your memory card.

Don't get me wrong; at times an optical viewfinder comes in handy — for example, when you're shooting outdoors on a sunny day, it's hard to see all but the brightest LCD display. Also, some folks find it easier to compose a photo using a traditional optical viewfinder. However, keep in mind that an LCD uses a lot of battery power to operate. Using an optical viewfinder whenever possible to frame and shoot your photos significantly extends your camera's battery life.

Interface

My use of the word *interface* might sound a little confusing to new owners of a digital camera who are also familiar with computers — you usually hear this word describing hard drives and CD-ROMs. However, an interface is simply a standard method for connecting one part of your computer to another, which is exactly what you must do to download the photographs that you've taken with your camera to your computer. Some camera interfaces can transfer an entire memory card worth of images in seconds, while others may take several minutes — and in this section, I'll describe each interface option you're likely to encounter.

■ **Serial (RS-232) connection.** The granddaddy of external connectors, practically every PC made has a serial port, so if your camera includes a serial cable you can use it with just about any computer. That's the good side. The bad side is the speed of a serial connection, which can transfer a typical one-megapixel image to your PC in 20 to 30 seconds. When you've got 40 or 50 images on your camera, that 30 seconds per shot can really add up! The serial connection is still the standard for low-cost cameras, although USB is fast becoming the norm.

Note

When I said "every PC" previously, note that I *didn't* say "every Macintosh"! If you're buying a camera for a Macintosh, it will likely need one of three types of connector: Mac serial (also called ADB), USB, or FireWire. A PC serial cable will *not* work with your Mac, so make sure you have the connection you need before you buy.

■ **USB.** If you're current with today's computer technology buzzwords, then you recognize USB (short for "Universal Serial Bus") right off the bat — it's one of the most popular connectors on today's computers. A USB connection can transfer an entire memory card's worth of 40 images to your PC or Mac computer within one to two minutes, making it a fast solution for a serious hobbyist. Cameras with USB are typically a little more expensive, and your operating system has to support it (Windows NT, older versions of Windows 95 and Mac's System 7, for example, can't use USB). Also, you'll have to install a USB adapter card in your PC if it didn't come with USB ports.

- **FireWire or IEEE-1394.** Faster than a speeding bullet, *FireWire* was developed especially to move huge files from external peripherals to a computer. You could easily download those 40 images (even in TIFF format) from your two-megapixel camera in just a few seconds. However, I'd actually have to label a FireWire connection as "overkill" for all but the most demanding amateur and professional photographers; for example, the Nikon D1 Digital SLR camera features FireWire, and it weighs in at a hefty $5,000. FireWire connectivity is most common on digital video cameras (also known as IEEE-1394 or, on Sony products, i.Link). Plus, only the latest Macintosh and PCs are likely to have FireWire onboard, so you'd probably have to buy an IEEE-1394 adapter card for your PC.

- **Infrared.** Does your laptop have an infrared (or IrDA, short for "Infrared Data Association") port? If so, a digital camera equipped with IrDA can transfer images to your laptop without a cable. An IrDA transfer is only slightly faster than a standard serial port connection, but it's easy — all you do is position the camera within range of the IrDA port on your laptop.

▲ Tip

One more thing: Remember how I mentioned that you can eject memory cards, floppy disks and memory sticks (and in some cases, even hard drives) from your computer? Most of these removable media have some sort of "reader" unit that you can buy that can download the images much faster than the standard serial connection. It's always a good idea to check whether your camera can use one of these — they can save you several minutes of time you'd otherwise spend waiting for a download to finish.

Metering

Here we are, back in the realm of the film camera again — *metering* refers to the measurement that you (or your camera) make to accommodate the available light in the environment. This measurement is used to help determine the exposure time used for a photograph. In the case of a typical point-and-shoot automatic camera, the metering system is totally automatic, and you have no control over it — for the typical shots taken by our Candid Snapshooter, automatic metering is fine.

On the other hand, manual metering — as with the flash control I mentioned before — has always been another tool of the serious amateur or professional photographer, and higher-priced digital cameras provide you with more than one way of gauging the light for a particular shot. For example, your camera can measure the light falling on the subject itself (which is assumed to be in the center of the frame), or the available light in the entire frame.

With manual metering, you can avoid a "washed out" or "murky" appearance to your shots — even in environments where a flash may be your primary light source.

Speed

Now let's consider the speed at which your new digital camera can capture motion — and the amount of time it takes to save an image and prepare itself for the next shot. Remember, one of the few advantages that a film camera has over a digital camera is the speed at which film can be exposed and advanced — because a digital camera uses an array of light-sensitive sensors, it takes longer to process the image, which then has to converted, compressed, named, and saved to the camera's memory card. This delay translates into additional seconds between the time that the camera takes an image and the moment the shutter can open again.

▲ Tip

Some digital cameras try to get around this delay with a feature called *continuous shutter* or *burst* mode — the camera uses a portion of its memory to store the raw image data from several shots in quick succession. With this continuous shutter feature turned on, you can typically take three or four shots within a second or two, but once the "burst" of photos has been taken you must give the camera the time it takes to process those shots. In other words, you're still going to wait those six seconds required to properly save the images, but you'll be doing it after the action is over. Most cameras with continuous shutter mode have a maximum limit of about 20 shots that you can take before processing must take place.

Unfortunately, digital cameras also lack the performance of a film camera when capturing motion — if your image is moving (or you move your arm while taking the picture), you can introduce blurring and distortion that you won't experience with a film camera. Higher-priced cameras have faster sensor arrays that can help reduce this problem, but a typical automatic digital camera is not going to be able to capture a car in motion during a NASCAR race. In fact, a much less expensive film camera loaded with 400-speed film will likely do a better job.

So what can you do? Check the shutter speeds listed in the specifications for cameras you're comparing — the faster the better for action shots, naturally. (Luckily, shutter speeds for digital cameras are similar to those used for film cameras, using the same unit of measurement.) Most manufacturers also provide comparisons between the speed of their image capture and the ISO speed rating used with today's film cameras, so it's possible to shop for a model with better performance. If action shots are your bread and butter, you'll also need a shutter priority control and a continuous shutter option — and you should be prepared to pay for these features, too!

Camera Controls

Buttons, buttons, buttons! In this section, I'll try to cover the major controls that are common on today's digital cameras. But first, I'd like to jump on the soapbox for a few seconds and point out two common problems I've encountered with today's digital camera controls:

■ **What's with these small buttons, anyway?** If you're evaluating a digital camera in person at a store (instead of checking out the specifications on a Web page), take a moment to make sure that you can quickly and easily manipulate the control buttons. One of the cameras I've used in the past had control buttons that Thomas Edison himself probably couldn't have handled on a good day — they were the size of a pencil point, and they were scattered in various spots all over the camera! I like buttons that are at least the size of a pencil eraser, and grouped in one spot.

■ **Multifunction isn't always good.** As with the familiar 35mm SLR film camera body, most of the more expensive digital cameras have separate buttons to set features such as the self-timer and flash. When you're in a hurry, separate buttons are better, because multifunction buttons might slow you down — for example, those separate buttons can help you make quick setting changes at a football game without missing the action you're there to shoot.

Okay, now that I've vented, the following is a list of the features I recommend for typical digital cameras — you'll find more detailed descriptions of most of these features elsewhere in this chapter, so if you don't understand something, feel free to flip back and read the specifics.

The minimum set

These features should be on every camera, including everything from point-and-shoot automatics to the most expensive digital SLR models:

■ A film counter and battery indicator

■ The shutter button

Not a very large list, is it? I did that for a reason: to illustrate that some of the digital cameras on the market for under $100 literally have *no other controls!* Naturally, only the most dedicated "point-and-shoot" photographer would be satisfied with this list; this is one reason why these cameras are usually marketed to kids. If you're looking for anything more than the bare minimum, I recommend that you give these "stocking stuffer" digital cameras a wide berth!

The standard set

Now let's move to a standard entry-level point-and-shoot that has some additional features — typical of a camera selling for less than $400. Besides the minimum set of controls, you would probably add:

■ A photo quality control (that controls compression, resolution, or both)

- A self-timer
- An LCD display
- A built-in flash with red-eye reduction
- Digital zoom

The deluxe set

Next, we'll add the features you'd find on a more expensive camera selling for more than $500 or so:

- Optical zoom
- A manual/automatic exposure control
- Resolution control

The ultimate set

Finally, here are the features you would add if money were no object while shopping:

- True manual focusing (with a lens mount for F-series lenses)
- Manual metering
- Manual exposure control
- An image format control
- Continuous shutter control
- External flash connector
- Remote control or shutter release

As you can see, the more money you spend, the more freedom you have to chart your own creative course with manual settings.

▲ Tip

If your camera uses an LCD menu to configure and control most of its features, I think that's certainly acceptable — however, as I said earlier, don't expect to fly through a series of photos that need different settings! You'll have to stop and move through the menu system to change flash and zoom settings, for example.

Other Features to Covet

Let's discuss additional features that may help you choose between cameras; because these "extras" can appear in cameras of all price ranges, you may find a particular model that offers a little something more for a similar price!

Audio

Why settle for recording the events in your life with just an image? With a camera that offers audio recording and playback, you can capture sound as well! For example, the Hewlett-Packard PhotoSmart 618 camera can record up to 45 seconds of sound for each image that you shoot. The sounds you record with the camera's built-in microphone are saved to the same memory card as your images (which means that your available space for photographs will decrease, so it pays to keep track of how many images remain on your card).

✏ Note

Are you thinking of recording the audio from a graduation ceremony or a couple's wedding vows with your camera? Keep in mind that a camera's microphone has very little range, so you won't be able to record sound farther than about two feet away. Instead, this feature is intended for you to add your own commentary to match your photographs.

Video

Besides the still images that we all want, many digital cameras can also capture full-motion video in MPEG or AVI format — notice I didn't say "audio" (most cameras with this feature can't record *synchronized* audio, which is more in the realm of a camcorder). Because a memory card really isn't suitable for storing high-quality video, you're usually limited to a few seconds of recording time, or your footage may be the size of a postage stamp when you view it on your computer. This is a neat feature, however, especially if you suddenly find yourself without your video camera and your baby takes her first step!

Onboard image management

This feature is one of the reasons why I've moved almost exclusively to the convenience of digital cameras — if your camera has an LCD screen, you probably can perform most of these functions:

- **Viewing all images stored in your memory card.**

- **Deleting one or more images.**

- **Organizing images into folders.**

- **Formatting the memory card.** By formatting the card, you erase all images, emptying it completely.

- **Adding a digital zoom.** As I mentioned earlier in the chapter, this is useful for enlarging the subject of an image (at the cost of some resolution).

- **Adding a border.** Your camera may enable you to add a border around the image before it's downloaded or printed.

- **Setting image brightness and contrast.** As with the brightness and contrast settings available on your computer monitor, you can lighten a photo that's too dark or enhance the contrast of the subject against the background.

- **Displaying a slide show with the images stored in your memory card.**

If you feel like I do, the more you can do with your digital camera *without* your computer, the better! The first generation of digital cameras usually required you to use the computer to handle these chores, but each year I've seen more and more sophisticated software built into the cameras themselves (some cameras actually have an "operating system" now, just like your computer). For example, the HP PhotoSmart 618 camera can even add the date and time, a line or two of text, or your company logo as a "watermark" behind your photos!

Software

Speaking of software, you should evaluate more than the onboard software that comes with your digital camera — most camera manufacturers provide you with all the programs you'll need to take full advantage of your new toy. These programs should include:

- **An image-downloading program.** This is standard equipment — after all, the camera manufacturer has to give you some way to get those images to your computer! However, some programs give you more features to boot — displaying all the images as thumbnails, perhaps, or providing conversion to another format after the download.

- **An image-editing program.** This is the jewel of a digital camera software suite — with the right image editor, you can actually improve your photographs in ways that no film photographer could ever imagine! Popular image editors include Adobe PhotoDeluxe and JASC Paint Shop Pro. I'll be showing you how to use Paint Shop Pro in Chapter 11.

- **An image display program.** These applications show you your images and enable you to print them or prepare them for e-mailing. Popular image display programs include Ulead Photo Explorer and ACDSee Viewer. I'll get into Photo Explorer in depth in Chapter 4.

Other Goodies You May Need

Finally, it's time to talk about the other goodies you may need along with your new digital camera — some of these are familiar to every film photographer, while others are demanded only within the digital world of ones and zeros.

- **Memory Card Reader.** If you recall, earlier in the chapter I likened downloading 40 high-resolution images over a serial connection to watching paint dry — if your camera doesn't offer a USB connection you can still speed things up by buying a memory card reader that *does*! To use a card reader, you eject the memory card from your camera, load it into the slot in the card reader and copy or move the images to your computer. Note that this also frees up your camera to accept another empty memory card while you are moving files to your computer — I use this trick myself with two memory cards, so I always have a fresh card in my camera, ready to shoot.

- **Tripod.** If you're serious about your photography — digital or film — a tripod is an essential purchase. With a digital camera, even the slightest movement of your arm can cause a blurred image, so a tripod helps steady the camera for portraits and scenic shots. Also, a tripod is a must-have if you'd like to try your hand at creative images using tricks such as time-lapse or double-exposure photography. Most cameras have a standard tripod mount, but it pays to check the camera's specifications before you buy.

- **Case.** You'd be surprised at how many folks buy a $700 digital camera and carry it around hanging from a cheap wrist strap! A case is a photographer's home base, carrying spare memory cards, filters, lenses, extra batteries, an AC adapter or battery charger — even a collapsible tripod. (Oh, and incidentally, it helps protect the camera, too.)

Tip

I personally recommend a camera case with removable partitions — they'll enable you to reconfigure the compartments inside the case to accept different camera bodies and different lenses as you update and improve your equipment. Also, make sure the case you choose has plenty of pouches and pockets for all the odd-shaped paraphernalia that surrounds the photographer.

- **Lens cloth.** Again, common sense here. You can pick up an inexpensive photographer's lens cloth at any photo shop for $4, and it helps protect your camera lenses from dust and dirt, as well as your LCD screen.

Warning

Don't even think about "polishing" your camera's lens with a paper towel, a tissue, or your shirt — you can damage the lens (and your reputation as the next Ansel Adams of digital photography).

- **Adapters, filters, and lenses.** If your digital camera can accept polarizing and colored filters or accessory lenses, I strongly recommend you try them out if you're interested in photography as an art form. (I'll be discussing more about specialty lenses throughout the book.)

- **Light meter.** Last but not least, a standard handheld light meter such as those used by film photographers can help achieve the same results for a digital photographer — it'll take some experimentation, but once you've learned to "match" a light level with an exposure and flash setting, you can eliminate errors and help guarantee a good shot in extreme lighting conditions. (Remember, experimentation with a digital camera won't cost you a cent in development or film!)

Summary

In this chapter, I covered your digital camera shopping list from A to Z. You learned about the features you should use for comparisons by evaluating the three most important criteria for a digital camera: your goals as a photographer, your level of experience, and your wallet. We also discussed the essential extras that every digital camera owner should pack (including the trusty camera case itself).

In the next chapter, I help you set up and prepare your camera for your first photo!

CHAPTER 3

Setting Up Your Camera

IN THIS CHAPTER
- Installing batteries and memory cards
- Installing the software
- Before you shoot . . .
- Connecting your camera

If you've just bought your digital camera and you'd like help in setting things up and connecting it to your computer, you'll find everything you need in this chapter. (On the other hand, if you're already been using your digital camera and you've downloaded plenty of photographs from your camera to your computer, you can skip this chapter.)

Note

In this chapter, I'll be using the Hewlett-Packard PhotoSmart C200 and C500 cameras to demonstrate procedures — however, you should be able to follow along with just about any typical "point-and-shoot" digital camera, no matter what brand.

Installing Batteries and Memory Cards

First things first — without batteries and a memory (also called a RAM) card, your new digital camera won't work. To test the operation of your camera, you need to install both.

Tip

Don't throw anything away yet! Just in case you've bought a defective camera, you'll need the box and packaging to return it. As a general rule, I keep computer hardware boxes for about a year. If you think that you may sell your camera in the future, it's an even better idea to hold onto the box and packaging indefinitely — hardware tends to sell much better when you can provide it in the original box.

Battery basics

Sure, I know that you've probably installed hundreds of batteries in your lifetime — so I won't be going over the procedure for installing them. However, I would like to stress the basic battery guidelines that every digital photographer should know.

■ **Use "high drain" or photo lithium batteries!** As I've mentioned already, digital cameras eat electricity like a toddler eats crackers. In a digital camera or other power-hungry electronic devices, "high drain" alkaline batteries such as Duracell Ultra and Energizer E² are worth the

higher cost you will pay compared to standard alkaline batteries. In the long run they will end up costing you about the same and you'll have to replace them around half as often. Photo lithium AA batteries are even better. In spite of their high initial cost, they end up costing less than most alkaline batteries per unit of energy. Photo lithium batteries last two to five times longer than standard alkaline batteries.

■ **Check the battery direction.** It happens to everyone — your camera doesn't seem to work and sits in your hands like an inert chunk of rock. If you've just changed your batteries, check how they're facing in the battery compartment. I'll bet at least one is facing in the wrong direction. (Luckily, this won't hurt anything.)

■ **Completely drain/discharge and then fully recharge batteries.** This helps avoid "memory effect" on rechargeable nickel cadmium (NiCad) or nickel metal hydride (NiMH) batteries. The term "memory effect" actually describes any voltage depression or capacity loss. In general, the loss of capacity is due to the battery being partially discharged and recharged repetitively — the problem also occurs when a rechargeable battery is allowed to sit unused for an extended period of time. A few full discharge/charge cycles generally restores the cell to normal. You can buy a charger with a "conditioning" cycle, which discharges the battery for you at a low rate. I recommend one of these models if you use standard NiMH batteries regularly. Be sure to check your digital camera manual to ensure that it supports rechargeable batteries.

■ **Plug your camera in while you download.** Because you'll normally be downloading to your computer with a handy wall socket nearby, make sure you plug in your AC adapter to conserve your batteries.

Installing a memory card

Once your batteries are in place and your camera has power, it may start chirping; your camera isn't being rude, it's simply telling you that it can't take photographs without a memory card! To load your memory card, follow these steps:

1. Open the memory card access door. Figure 3.1 shows the memory card access door on the PhotoSmart C500 — if you need help identifying or opening the door on your camera, check the camera manual for more information.

2. Locate the memory card slot and insert the card. Most cameras have an arrow indicating the label side of the card, and the connector on your memory card should face toward the body of the camera. Figure 3.2 shows the memory card in the proper orientation for the HP PhotoSmart C500 camera. Push the card into the body of the camera until it clicks into place.

Warning

If the memory card does not snap into place after you've applied fingertip pressure, *do not attempt to force it into place!* You could damage the internal connectors, or even break the memory card. Check your camera's manual for the proper alignment of your card in the camera's slot. Naturally, you should also keep them away from liquids, and handle them with the same care that you use with a floppy disk.

3. Close the memory card access door.

4. Format the memory card. Like a new hard drive, a brand-new memory card will require

Figure 3.1 I've opened the memory card access door on the side of the PhotoSmart C500.

Figure 3.2 Ready to push the memory card into place.

formatting before you can use it. I'll cover this procedure later in this chapter.

Removing a memory card

To unload a memory card, follow these steps:

1. Open the memory card access door.

2. Press the memory card eject button (or lever) to eject the card.

Warning

Never eject a memory card while the camera is turned on — you can lose the data on the card, or perhaps even damage the card itself.

3. Close the memory card access door.

Installing the Software

As I mentioned in Chapter 2, most digital cameras will come with several programs to help you download and edit your images — some also come with software you can use to print your photographs or send them through e-mail. Before you can use this software, however, you have to install it. To demonstrate the process, I'll show you how to install the software suite that accompanies the PhotoSmart C200 camera—in ten easy steps.

1. Load the CD-ROM that you received with your camera. Under Windows 95 and 98, the installation program should start automatically and display the screen shown in Figure 3.3. Click Next to continue.

2. Choose the image programs you want to install. To install a program, click the checkbox next to the name to enable it—an X appears to indicate that it has been selected. Because I'll be using all three of these programs to demonstrate procedures throughout the book, I strongly recommend that you install all three—however, the only program that's absolutely required is the C200 Photo Imaging Software. Figure 3.4 illustrates this screen with all three programs selected. Click Next to continue.

3. Confirm your choices. The installation program gives you a chance to confirm your selections, as shown in Figure 3.5. If everything is correct, click Next to continue. To make a change, click Back to return to previous installation screens.

4. Agree to the software license. To continue with the installation process, you must first agree to the terms of the HP software license

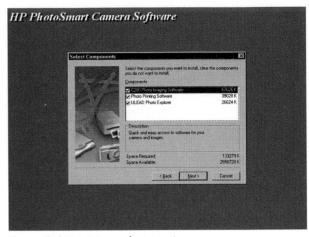

Figure 3.4 Decisions, decisions!

agreement. Read the terms carefully, and then click Yes to continue if you agree.

5. Select a location. The installation program enables you to choose the location where the software will be saved, as shown in Figure 3.6. I recommend that you use the default location that's provided, but if you need to change it, click the Browse button and select a new location on your hard drive. Click Next to continue.

6. Confirm your choices. If you're satisfied with the location you picked, click Next to begin

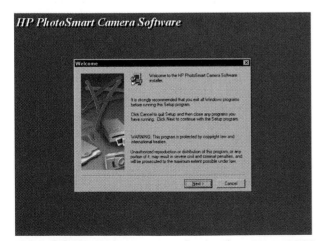

Figure 3.3 The Welcome screen for the PhotoSmart C200 camera installation program.

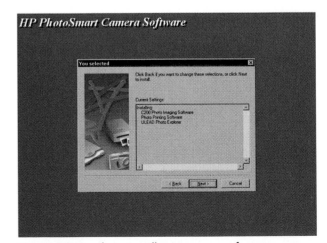

Figure 3.5 Ready to install our camera software.

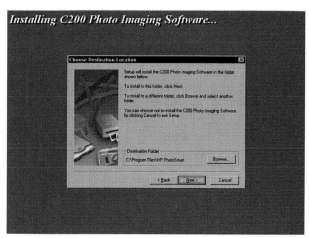

Figure 3.6 Choose a home for your files.

copying files. To make a change, click Back to return to the previous installation screen.

If you decided to install the Ulead Photo Explorer program, you'll see a separate Welcome screen for it after the HP programs have been copied; click Next to continue with the following steps.

7. Agree to the software license. To continue with the installation process, you must first agree to the terms of the Ulead Systems software license agreement. Read the terms carefully, and then click Yes to continue if you agree.

8. Select a location. Again, I recommend that you use the default location that's provided, but if you need to change it click the Browse button and select a new location for the Ulead Photo Explorer program on your hard drive. Click Next to continue.

9. Confirm your choices. If you're satisfied with the location you picked, click Next to begin copying files. To make a change, click Back to return to previous installation screen.

10. You're done! Click Finish after the completion message has been displayed.

Installing software is a breeze with Windows 98. Believe me — I remember the Stone Age of computers!

Before You Shoot . . .

You should take care of a number of preparations before you begin taking photographs with your new digital camera. This section provides you with a checklist of guidelines for what to do before you shoot.

Formatting the memory card

If your camera uses a memory card and you've just loaded it for the first time, or if you've just bought a brand-new memory card for an existing camera, you may have to *format* it before you can use it. Formatting prepares the memory chips inside your memory card to accept image data, much like the formatting procedure used on a floppy disk or a hard drive prepares them to store data files.

The procedure you follow to format your memory card will vary depending on the camera, so check your manual for step-by-step instructions.

Select a photo quality

As I mentioned in Chapter 2, most digital cameras on the market today feature more than one photo quality — the higher the quality, the lower the compression setting. (On some cameras, selecting a different photo quality also changes the final image resolution.) Therefore, selecting a higher image quality results in a larger image, which takes up additional space on your memory card. It's a tradeoff — you can have a larger number of lower-quality images, or a smaller number of higher-quality images.

"But why do I have to choose a photo quality now, before I even take a photo?" Good question, and here's the answer: On *some* cameras, you must set the photo quality for an entire set of images before you take your first shot! Therefore, if you take a great photo at standard photo quality, all the other images you take on that memory card must also be standard photo quality — naturally, once you've download the images and deleted them from the card, you can again select a new photo quality. It's important to remember that you can always reduce file quality and size at a later time with your image editor, if necessary, but you can never increase the quality of a lower-quality image.

Check your camera's manual to see if you can set photo quality "on the fly" for each image you take — if you can, you don't have to worry. Even if you don't have to choose a photo quality for an entire card's worth of images at once, it's still a good idea to decide what resolution you'll use for most shots, and set your camera accordingly.

The procedure for selecting a photo quality setting is different for every camera model — for example, there's a separate Photo Quality button on the HP PhotoSmart C500 camera (a convenient feature), but you may have to use an LCD menu to set quality on your model.

Configure your flash

Like your photo quality setting, it's also a good idea to configure your flash if your camera offers multiple settings — this can save you time while you're shooting.

I use the red-eye reduction flash setting on my cameras, but many digital photographers don't like the two flashes that occur with this setting on. (The first flash is designed to acclimate the eye for the second flash, which goes off when the picture is actually taken.) Red-eye reduction does take a second or two more, and if your subjects are usually moving — or, in the case of a happy toddler, *ready* to move — it may be a better idea to turn red-eye reduction off as a default.

◩ **Cross-Reference**

In Chapter 7, I discuss tips and tricks for flash lighting.

Practice holding your camera

Okay, I know that sounds really dumb. However, holding your camera correctly — and I'm not talking about leaving your thumb over the lens — actually makes a big difference in digital photography. Why? Recall what I've said so far about the amount of time it takes for your digital camera to take an exposure, and how moving objects tend to blur. The logical result is a blurred image if the photographer is moving as well!

For example, check out the two images I've taken in Figures 3.7 and 3.8 — both taken of the same

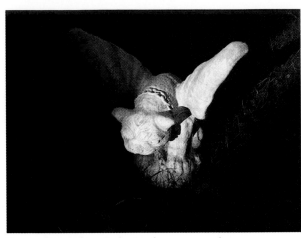

Figure 3.7 A friend of mine from my garden.

subject at the same time of day. See if you can guess which one was taken while I was moving the camera? (And I wasn't jumping up and down, either; it only takes a subtle motion to ruin a shot.)

So, how do you maintain the steadiness you need for a good digital photograph? Remember the two golden rules of camera grip:

■ If you're holding the camera, keep your arm locked against your body.

■ If you're using the optical viewfinder, press the camera lightly against your forehead.

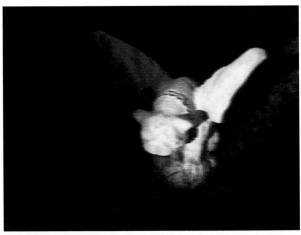

Figure 3.8 Not looking that good — of course, I was moving the camera.

Of course, a digital camera can be held either horizontally or vertically, just like a film camera, and you'll find that you greatly reduce the chance of a blurred image in either orientation by simply following the preceding two rules.

▲ Tip

If you're using an LCD viewfinder, things get a little more difficult — that's why I recommend that every digital photographer pick up a tripod (you can find them at a discount store for around $30). With a collapsible tripod, you can be ready to capture an important image in less than a minute, and you can use your digital camera's LCD viewfinder without worrying.

Learn those controls!

Finally, take an evening and completely familiarize yourself with the controls on your camera. Sooner or later, I can *guarantee* you that you're going to be presented with a great moment that cries out for a candid photograph — and in my experience, that moment usually passes quickly, giving you just a few seconds to capture it!

With practice, you can have your digital camera powered up and ready to go — even with a flash adjustment or a manual focus — within five or fewer seconds. To meet that kind of time limit, you need to know the location of each button and control on your camera. (Again, I'll say that more expensive cameras shy away from controls that operate multiple functions for this reason — you can make adjustments quickly, often without even looking at the camera itself.)

Connecting Your Camera

Once you've taken enough shots to fill your camera's memory card, you'll need to connect your camera to your computer to download the images. (Naturally, if your camera uses an infrared connection, cables aren't even required.) In this section, I'll show you how to make a serial and USB connection.

Connecting a serial camera cable

Follow these steps to connect a serial camera cable:

1. Locate a 9-pin serial port on the front or back of your computer. Figure 3.9 illustrates a serial port.

2. Align the 9-pin connector on the end of your camera cable with the serial port. Note that the connector can go on only one way.

3. When the connector is correctly aligned, push it in firmly.

4. Tighten the connector by turning the knobs on the connector clockwise. Some connectors use screws instead; you need a very small screwdriver to tighten these connectors.

5. Connect the other end of the cable to your camera's serial port.

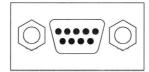

Figure 3.9 Many digital cameras use the serial port to transfer data.

Connecting a USB camera cable

Follow these steps to connect a USB camera cable:

1. Connect the USB cable to your camera's USB port.

Working with a Single Serial Port

Because some computers only have one serial port — and the serial port is also commonly used for an external modem or serial mouse — you may be faced with a problem. If your serial port is already used, consider adding an adapter card to your computer that provides more serial ports. Alternately, you can add an internal modem that doesn't use the serial port (or, if your computer has USB connections, you can buy a USB modem) or purchase a memory card reader so you can use your memory card with your computer. Also, many computers actually have two serial ports, but the second one isn't connected to the outside of the case; before you buy anything, check your computer to determine if you can add a second port. (A local computer repair shop can help you if you've never ventured inside your computer's case.)

2. Depending on the camera you're using, you may have to run your image download program before you connect the USB cable to your computer. Your camera manual should tell you if this is necessary.

3. Plug the other end of the camera USB cable into a USB port on your computer—note that the connector can go on only one way.

4. On some cameras, Windows will recognize the camera automatically and load your image download program for you.

Summary

We covered the preparations that every new owner of a digital camera needs to make in this chapter: installing batteries, memory cards and software, a number of suggestions for digital photographers who want to take the best possible pictures, and connecting the camera to the computer when it's time to download images.

In the next chapter, you'll learn how to process your images after you've taken them.

General Digital Photography Techniques

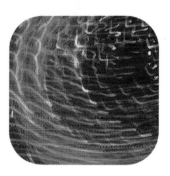

Processing Digital Images

IN THIS CHAPTER
- Downloading your images
- Viewing images on your computer
- Cataloging your images

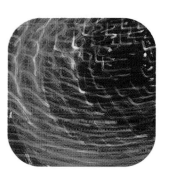

As I mentioned in Chapter 1, digital cameras are popular for two reasons: the convenience they offer and the money you save. Although you don't need to buy film or visit the development lab, you still need to process your images — call it digital development, if you like.

This chapter walks you through a typical digital development session. First, I demonstrate how to download images from an HP PhotoSmart C200 digital camera, and then we'll view the images you've taken on your computer. Finally, I discuss a number of methods you can use to catalog your images for easy retrieval in the future.

Downloading Your Images

The exact process that you'll follow to download images from your digital camera to your computer will vary somewhat, due to the following:

- **The software you're using.** Typically, the manufacturer of a camera includes a proprietary downloading application.

- **The type of connection to your camera.** As I discussed in Chapter 2, the connection can be made over a serial, USB or FireWire cable, an infrared link, a floppy disk, a PCMCIA card, or a memory card reader.

In fact, you may not even need to do anything special to download images because some cameras, such as the HP PhotoSmart 618 and 912, actually behave like external disk drives when connected to a computer. You can copy or move files directly from the camera to the computer's hard drive by using Windows Explorer.

Luckily, however, the general steps involved in downloading images are practically universal, so you should be able to follow along no matter what type of camera you own. Make sure, of course, that you read your camera's manual and the documentation for your downloading program first! Reading this information will familiarize you with any special settings you may have to change or additional steps you may have to perform for your specific model.

Once you're ready to download your images, follow these steps:

1. Connect your camera to your computer. Figure 4.1 shows my digital camera connected to the serial port on my computer. Remember, use an AC power supply with your camera while downloading to conserve your battery power.

> **Note**
>
> If you're using a memory card reader (or other removable media, such as a floppy or PCMCIA card), eject the media and load it in the corresponding drive that you've installed on your computer. If you're using an infrared link, turn your camera on and move it close to the infrared port on your computer.

2. Turn the camera on. On the C200 this is done by opening the lens cover. Some cameras can automatically detect that they're connected and will show a message on their status display.

3. Run the downloading software. With the PhotoSmart C200 camera, the installation software places an icon for the C200 Photo Imaging Software on your Windows desktop; click this icon to run the program. The main screen shown in Figure 4.2 appears.

4. For the HP PhotoSmart C200 camera, you click Unload Camera. The program displays the Camera Unload dialog box shown in Figure 4.3, where you can set unload options.

Figure 4.1 A HP PhotoSmart C200 digital camera connected through a serial link, ready to download.

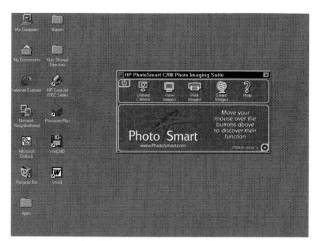

Figure 4.2 The initial screen displayed by the PhotoSmart Photo Imaging Suite.

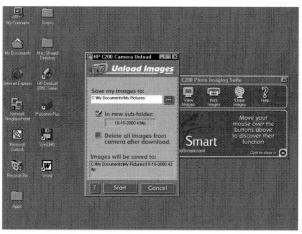

Figure 4.3 Selecting unload options before I begin downloading my images.

5. Set the unload options. By default, the program saves your images in a subfolder called My Pictures within the familiar My Documents folder—however, if you want to specify a new target location on your system, click the Browse button to select it. To help keep your images organized, the program also creates a new directory based on the current date and time (you can turn this off by disabling the "In new sub-folder" checkbox, which places everything in My Pictures). Finally, you can also automatically delete all of the images once they've been downloaded by enabling the Delete all images from camera after download checkbox—a handy feature that saves you a step later, because otherwise you'll have to delete them from the camera's LCD menu or format the memory card. Once you've set all the options as you like, click Start to continue.

6. Confirm the creation of the new folder. If you enabled the "In new sub-folder" option in the previous step, the program requests confirmation before creating the new directory; click Yes to continue.

▲ **Tip**

To avoid this extra mouse click in the future, enable the "Don't remind me again" checkbox before you click Yes — the program will no longer display this confirmation dialog box in the future and will automatically create the new folder.

7. Watch each photo as it's downloaded. The program displays a thumbnail image of the picture as it's being downloaded—don't worry, this thumbnail is not actual size! It's just for your reference, and only the full-size image is saved to disk.

8. Once all of your images have been downloaded from the camera, the program shows you the completion dialog box shown in Figure 4.4. Click Close to return to the program's main screen.

Figure 4.4 All done! The images you've taken with your camera are now on your hard drive.

9. Turn off the camera. Closing the lens cover on the C200 turns the camera off.

10. Disconnect your camera from your computer. If you don't need your computer's serial port for anything else, I recommend that you simply leave the cable connected—this will make it easy to plug the camera in the next time you're ready to download.

Viewing Images on Your Computer

Once the images are on your computer, you should be able to use any image editor to look at them—for example, Adobe Photoshop or JASC Paint Shop Pro are two popular programs. However, your camera's manufacturer may have provided you with an image-viewing program along with the downloading software—if so, there's no need to install another program to see those beautiful photographs.

For example, follow these steps to view your downloaded images with the PhotoSmart Photo Imaging Suite:

1. Run the Suite. If the Suite isn't running, click the C200 Photo Imaging Software icon on your Windows desktop.

2. Click View Images. The program runs Ulead Photo Explorer, which displays the screen shown in Figure 4.5. Each photograph that you downloaded is represented by a thumbnail image.

▲ **Tip**

By default, Photo Explorer uses 80 × 80 thumbnails. If the thumbnails are too small (making them hard to see) or too large (forcing you to scroll through several pages of images), you can adjust the thumbnail size — click the Change Thumbnail Size drop-down list box on the toolbar and choose a different size. You can also expand the size of the thumbnails by removing the frame that surrounds them — click the View menu and choose the Disable Slide Frame option.

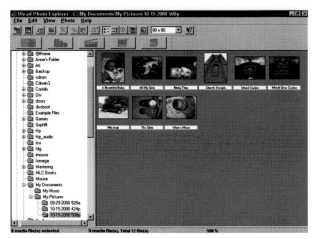

Figure 4.5 Viewing images with Ulead Photo Explorer.

3. Click an individual image. To view a picture at its regular size, double-click the desired thumbnail. Photo Explorer enlarges the image.

▲ **Tip**

By default, the program selects an image size that comfortably fits within your screen resolution. However, if you're running Windows at a high resolution (say 1,152 × 864, as I do), you can expand the image. To zoom in, click the image once or click the zoom-in icon at the top of the window. (It looks like a magnifying glass with a plus sign inside.) To zoom out, click the zoom-out icon (with the minus sign) at the top of the window.

Photo Explorer provides a number of other features that you may find useful while viewing images:

■ **Moving to another folder.** To move from one folder to another, use the folder tree on the left pane of the Photo Explorer window—it works much like the Windows Explorer. Click a folder to open it—if it contains image files that Photo Explorer recognizes, the program automatically displays them. You can also click a plus sign next to a folder to expand it and click the minus sign next to a folder to close it.

■ **Converting a file to another image format.** I've already discussed image formats in Chapter 1. Although the JPEG format produced by most digital cameras is a good pick for e-mailing, archiving, and Web publishing, you may need to convert an image for a specific application. See Chapter 10 for more information on different image formats. Display the image you want to convert, and then click the Photo menu and select the Convert menu item to display the dialog box shown in Figure 4.6. In most cases, you'll simply want to choose the new format in the Convert File Format to drop-down list box — I discuss data types and resampling later in the book, but they're usually not required if you simply want to convert to another format. Click OK to convert the file.

▲ Tip

Take my word for it — you don't want to overwrite your existing file with the converted file, and you don't want to delete the original file! Accidents *will* happen — so it's always a good idea to enable the Save in another subfolder checkbox. (Click the Browse button to specify the location for the new file.) Also, I strongly recommend that you don't enable the "Delete original files" checkbox unless you know exactly how the new converted image will look!

■ **Copy an image to the clipboard.** Would you like to insert one of the images you've taken into a document created with another application, such as Microsoft Word? Display the image you want to copy, and then click the Edit menu and select the Copy command. (You can also use the familiar Windows shortcut key sequence Ctrl+C.)

Cataloging Your Images

Sooner or later, the cataloging bug is likely to bite you. You may decide to organize your pictures after you've downloaded your first set of images or after you've collected a year's worth of photographs. Many image editing and image viewing programs can build a thumbnail catalog for you — some can automatically update your catalog when the contents of a specific folder change, such as when you add or delete images. For example, Figure 4.7 illustrates another of my favorite image editing programs, Paint Shop Pro, with a thumbnail catalog that it creates.

Even if you don't yearn for an orderly arrangement for your photos — I'll be the first to admit I'm not an orderly person — you should build a catalog of your images for two very good reasons:

■ **It's easier to search and sort your images.** If you need a particular photo from your collection, an image catalog makes it easier to identify that one image out of hundreds. The name of the image may not always be indicative of the subject, but with a thumbnail catalog you can pick it out easily.

■ **It's easy to compare images.** For example, let's assume that you have dozens of pictures of your child playing baseball, and now you want to create a holiday card featuring your child. Without

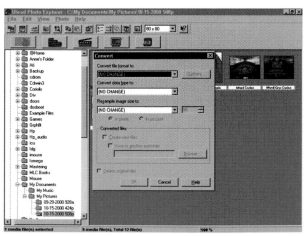

Figure 4.6 Converting an image by using Ulead Photo Explorer.

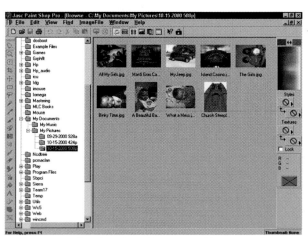

Figure 4.7 A thumbnail catalog created by Paint Shop Pro.

a thumbnail catalog, you could spend an hour laboriously opening and closing an image editor to compare one shot against the others — or, you could open all of them in your catalog and pick out the perfect photograph in seconds!

Ulead Photo Explorer takes the idea of a thumbnail catalog one step farther with a really neat feature that I've used often — the program can create an online thumbnail catalog for your Web page! Visitors to your Web catalog can click a thumbnail, and the full-size image will be displayed in their browsers. These online catalogs are used for everything from Web product catalogs to "virtual" scenic vacation tours.

Follow these steps to make an HTML page with your thumbnails, ready for your Web site:

1. Run the Suite. If the Suite isn't running already, click the C200 Photo Imaging Software icon on your Windows desktop.

2. Click View Images. The program runs Ulead Photo Explorer.

3. Select the desired folder. If the images you want to catalog are not in the current folder, use the Explorer pane at the left side of the window to open the right folder.

 Tip

Using the Explorer pane, you can also drag and drop image files from another location into the folder that you'll use to create your Web catalog.

4. Select the desired images. Click once on each image you want to add in the folder — or, to select all of the images, click the Edit menu and choose the Select All menu item.

5. Display the Output HTML Thumbnails dialog box. From the File menu, click Output HTML Thumbnails to display the dialog box shown in Figure 4.8.

 Tip

You can click the Preview button to view the page at any stage of the process.

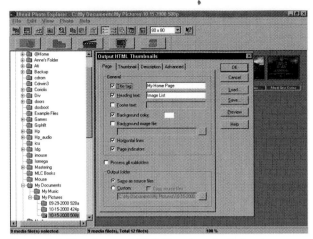

Figure 4.8 The Output HTML Thumbnails dialog box.

6. Set the Page options. A number of options are available; most of them will work fine with the defaults. However, you'll probably want to personalize your page with your own title, heading, and footer.

7. Set the Thumbnail options. Click the Thumbnail tab to set the number, size, and arrangement of the thumbnail images on the Web page. It's a good idea to set the Thumbnail file format option to Auto, which accommodates cameras that produce both GIF and JPEG images.

 Tip

If you enable the "Hyperlink to source file" option, clicking one of the thumbnail images automatically displays the full-size photo. Naturally, the full-size photos will have to be uploaded to your Web site along with the Web catalog files.

8. Set the Description options. Click the Description tab to add a descriptive caption for each image with information such as the file name, file size, format, and resolution. The caption can be aligned in a number of different ways.

9. Set the Advanced options. Finally, click the Advanced tab to add another HTML file as a

header or footer or change the dimensions, colors, and background used by the program to create the image table.

10. Preview your work. If you haven't already, click Preview to see what the page will look like — Photo Explorer loads your browser and displays the page. This makes it easy to change an option or two before you create the final files. Figure 4.9 shows a preview of my Web image catalog.

11. Ready to go? Then click OK and sit back and relax while Photo Explorer creates the files, ready for uploading to your Web site.

Unless you specified otherwise, the program saves the files in the same directory where the original images are stored.

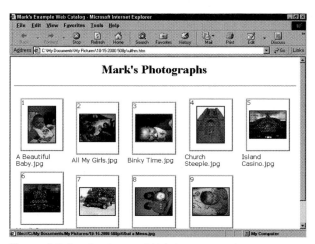

Figure 4.9 Previewing my Web image catalog.

Chapter 5 covers everything you need to know to print your digital photographs.

Summary

In this chapter, you learned how to download your images from your camera to your computer's hard drive, and you viewed them by using Ulead Photo Explorer. I also showed you how to catalog your images by using Ulead Photo Explorer, and you created an online image catalog for your Web site.

 # Printing Your Images

IN THIS CHAPTER
- Configuring printer options

- Setting orientation

- Selecting and printing images

- Who needs a PC, anyway?

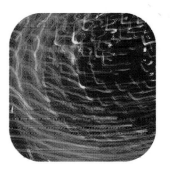

Although I'll be showing you many applications and uses for your digital photographs in this book, most folks have one primary use for their digital images: creating the same type of photo prints that you'd receive from a traditional development lab. Any inkjet printer capable of photo-quality output can do the job, but a number of tips and tricks will help you produce the best possible prints.

This chapter demonstrates how to print a digital photograph by using the HP PhotoSmart Photo Printing application, but I'll also cover what you need to know about paper and printer settings—and I'll also show you how you can use the HP PhotoSmart printer to produce prints directly from your memory card—no downloading from your camera to your computer is necessary with this new technology!

Configuring Printer Options

Before you load a single sheet of paper into your printer, it's important to configure your printer with the proper settings. Without choosing the correct print quality, paper type, color hue, and color intensity, I can practically guarantee you that your first attempts at printing your digital photographs will be disappointing—no matter how beautiful the image, and no matter how much you spent on your camera and printer.

Note

The settings I discuss in this section should apply to virtually any photo-quality printer, so don't skip this material just because your printer was manufactured by another company. Read on . . . you can't produce a great print without configuring your printer!

Print quality

Today's inkjet printers offer at least two *print quality* modes, and most provide three settings. Print quality determines:

- **How good the image looks.** Different printers use different methods to control print quality, but most printers will change the number of dots

that make up a pixel or the number of colors printed per dot, according to the quality you've selected. Some printers even reduce the number of pixels in the image (sometimes called *dots per inch*). Figure 5.1 illustrates two versions of the same image: one is printed at 600×600 dpi (right), while the other is printed at 300×300 dpi (left). You can see that the image quality suffers dramatically at a lower dpi setting.

- **How long the image takes to print.** The higher the quality setting you select, the longer the printer usually takes to produce the image.

- **How much ink is used to print.** The higher the quality setting you select, the more ink the printer will use to produce the image.

As an example, most Hewlett-Packard printers produce output by using one of three print quality settings:

- **EconoFast/Draft.** You should use this quality mode for draft work—for instance, a rough draft of a document or a quick copy of a Web page for future reference. Naturally, you should never use EconoFast or Draft mode to print a digital photograph unless you're trying to save ink and appearance isn't important.

- **Normal.** The default setting on most printers, Normal provides the best compromise between quality and speed. I've used Normal for printing digital photographs before, but only copies for friends. Again, you won't get the best possible image your printer can deliver.

- **Best.** Bingo! Use Best mode for printing any of your digital photographs where appearance is

Figure 5.1 Some printers drop the dpi of a printed image in draft mode.

most important—it results in the highest level of detail and the best color reproduction. However, give your printer extra time to print an image in Best mode. Figure 5.2 illustrates the Print Quality dialog box for my HP DeskJet printer.

Paper type

Next, consider the type of paper you're using to produce your prints—your inkjet printer probably comes with presets for several different types and sizes of paper, each of which may result in subtle differences in color and detail. We're mostly interested in two of them:

■ **Plain paper.** Your printer's paper type is probably set to plain paper by default. Plain paper is fine for printing rough drafts (often in conjunction with EconoFast/Draft or Normal print quality). Plain paper is not a good choice for your final print, however, because the image will lose detail, brightness, and color accuracy; the ink from your printer tends to soak into plain paper, and the colors are likely to blur or subtly change hue. You can use plain inkjet paper, and recycled paper works fine.

■ **Glossy or Photo paper.** Although glossy photo paper is significantly more expensive than regular inkjet paper, the results that it provides (in league with Best print quality, of course) are nothing short of spectacular! Ink doesn't soak into the glossy surface of photo paper, so there's no loss of detail and no blurring, and colors tend to stay bright and accurate.

▲ Tip

The glossy appearance of photo paper also lends to the "real film print" appearance of a digital photograph, too — in fact, some manufacturers of photo paper even add a watermark that looks like the printing on the back of traditional film prints!

Figure 5.3 illustrates the Paper Type control on my HP inkjet printer.

By the way, you're certainly not limited to the "traditional" 8½ × 11-inch format for your glossy photo paper—paper manufacturers, such as Hewlett-Packard, also produce photo paper in 4 × 6 formats, as well as glossy greeting card and postcard papers. (If you happen to have only 8½ × 11-inch paper and you want smaller prints, however, you can always print more than one image on the page and cut them later, as I describe later in this chapter.)

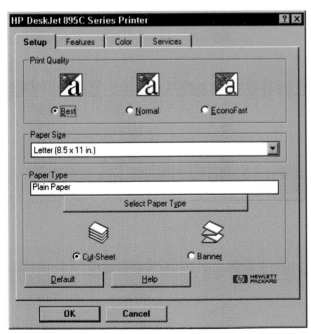

Figure 5.2 Selecting Best print quality mode for my HP printer.

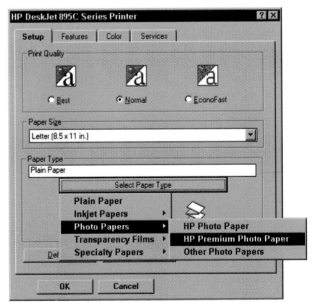

Figure 5.3 Selecting the proper paper type is important for producing the best prints.

Color intensity

Finally, you can use a setting called *color intensity* to enhance your printed photographs. Although the manufacturer of your printer may call this setting by another name (such as *brightness* or *image intensity*), the idea is simple: lighter images use less ink, and darker images use more. A change in color intensity can dramatically change the appearance of the printed image, much like changing the brightness setting on your computer monitor.

If you're using an HP inkjet printer, it may offer a feature called ColorSmart that can automatically choose the correct color intensity to most closely match the image as it's displayed on your monitor — it's a good idea to leave ColorSmart enabled unless you feel that you must make manual adjustments.

▲ Tip

Your printer may also be able to print an image in grayscale, which can help you produce a quick "black and white" print without actually reducing the number of colors or converting the image to grayscale — two tasks that would otherwise demand that you run your image editor.

In Figure 5.4, I'm making a manual adjustment to the color intensity setting on my HP printer.

Setting Orientation

Before you print an image, you may have to change its *orientation* — whether the length of the image is

facing horizontally or vertically. In the world of printers, you've probably seen orientation referred to as *portrait* or *landscape*. Portrait is the default, with the length of the image printed vertically, while an image printed in landscape mode has the length printed horizontally.

Portrait mode is a printing default for a good reason — most of the pages from your word processor are printed this way — but it's not necessarily the best default for printing photographs. Most photographers take images in landscape mode, with the body of the camera resting horizontally in their hands. Therefore, unless you change the orientation of a landscape image before you print it, it may not all fit on a portrait page (unless the program automatically resizes it).

To change your printer's orientation for an image before you print it, follow these steps:

1. Click File within your image editor or printing program and then select Print from the menu.

2. Click the Properties button that appears on the Print dialog box to display your printer's settings.

3. Choose Landscape orientation and click OK.

4. Print as usual.

▲ Tip

If you're printing more than one image on a page, you may need to change the orientation of the image instead. Most image-printing programs and image editors will let you *rotate* an image by 90 or 180 degrees, which permanently changes its orientation. Don't forget to save the new image to disk before you exit from the program!

Selecting and Printing Images

In the previous chapter, I showed you how to view the images you downloaded — at this point, you've probably decided which images you want to print, you've loaded the proper paper, and you've set the right printer options. As an example of the software you'll use to make your prints, I'll use the HP PhotoSmart Photo Printing program that accompanies the HP line of cameras.

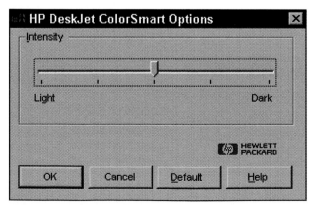

Figure 5.4 Color intensity determines the amount of ink that's used by the printer to produce an image.

To select and print your digital photographs, follow these steps:

1. **Run the program.** Click the HP Photo Printing icon on your Windows desktop. The program displays the window shown in Figure 5.5.

2. **Load your images.** Click the Open Files button in the program's toolbar to display the Open dialog box, and navigate to the location where your images are saved. You can see a preview of any image by selecting it. To pick multiple photographs, hold down the Shift or Ctrl key while you click. Once you've high-lighted the files you want to load, click Open to continue, and the images will appear in the left pane of the window.

3. **Select one or more images.** Click a thumbnail image to select it for addition to a print or album page—note that you can add more than one photo to a page by holding down the Ctrl key while you click. The program indicates that a photo has been selected by highlighting the thumbnail with a blue border, as shown in Figure 5.6.

Tip

Digital photographers that I talk to often make the mistake of sizing an image too large — remember, if it's a fairly low-resolution photograph (under one megapixel, for example), it probably won't look good "blown up" to fit a page as an 8 × 10. *Simply increasing the resolution of an image with an image editor does not preserve the*

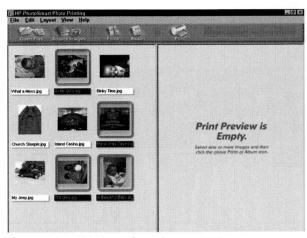

Figure 5.6 Highlighting four photos to print.

detail! Instead, print four of those low-resolution images on that same page as 3½ × 5 prints, and they'll look great — and you'll save that expensive glossy photo paper as well!

4. **Click the Prints button on the toolbar.** The program displays the Prints dialog box you see in Figure 5.7.

5. **Choose a layout.** Scroll through the different layouts displayed in the window to choose the one you want—you can **see** both the number of images that will fit on a page and the size of the images. To change the dimensions of the paper you'll be using, click the

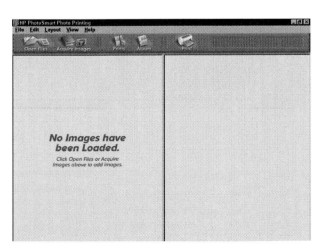

Figure 5.5 The HP PhotoSmart Photo Printing program.

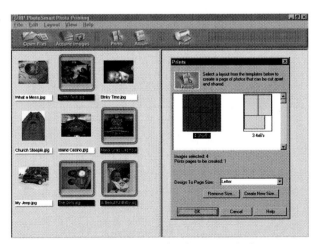

Figure 5.7 Selecting a layout for the printed photos.

DesignTo Page Size drop-down list box and choose the correct paper size. After you've decided which layout you want to use, click it once to highlight it and click OK, and the program will show you a preview of the page on the right pane of the window.

6. Click the Print button on the toolbar. This displays the standard Windows Print dialog box shown in Figure 5.2. If you haven't set your printer configuration as I described earlier in the chapter, do it now by clicking Properties!

7. Click OK to begin printing.

△ Tip

Need to cut separate images from a single page? Do what I do, and either buy an office-grade paper cutter that can handle thick paper, or visit your local copy center and use theirs! Even with a clearly-defined border, it's difficult to cut a photo by using scissors.

Who Needs a PC, Anyway?

I introduced the new generation of memory card–ready inkjets in Chapter 1 when I mentioned the HP PhotoSmart P1000 printer. These models can print without a connection to your computer. Printers like the HP PhotoSmart can accept both CompactFlash and SmartMedia memory cards — or if your camera supports the HP JetSend infrared protocol, you can print images without even removing the memory card. (Talk about the ultimate in convenience!)

You may be wondering how you can select specific images to print from a memory card without a computer monitor; the HP PhotoSmart printer creates the same type of thumbnail catalog that I mentioned in Chapter 4. By printing a catalog index, you can easily determine which images you want to print directly and which will require editing or cropping within your image-editing program.

Follow these steps to print images directly from your camera's memory card by using the HP PhotoSmart printer:

1. Turn your printer on and load it with the desired paper. (As I mentioned earlier, this is typically glossy photo paper, unless you're printing an index page, where you should use plain or inkjet paper.)

2. Plug the memory card into the matching slot on your printer — the edge with the connectors should go first.

3. As soon as the printer has finished reading the contents of the card and displays the completion message on the printer LCD, press the CANCEL/NO button on the printer's front panel until the display reads "ALL PHOTOS – 1 copy – Index." HP PhotoSmart printers have two paper trays, one for 4×6 media and the other for standard $8\frac{1}{2} \times 11$-inch papers. Make sure that the 4×6 paper tray is not engaged and that you have one or two sheets of plain paper loaded in the bottom tray. Press the PRINT button to print an index page.

4. Use the thumbnail images on the index page to select the photos you'd like to print.

5. Press the Choose Photos button until the index number of the first photo that you want to print appears. (To print all of the pictures, simply choose the All option.) Press the OK button to mark the photo.

6. If you're printing only selected images, repeat Step 5 until you've marked all the images you want to print.

7. Once you've marked all the images you'd like to print, click OK.

8. Choose the desired size for your photographs by pressing the Photo Size button until the proper size appears on the display — note that this is not necessarily the same as your paper size!

9. Press the COPIES button until the proper number of copies you want to print of each photo appears on the display.

10. Remove any remaining plain paper from the bottom tray and insert photo paper.

11. Press the PRINT button to start printing your photos.

Summary

This chapter covered the printing of your digital photographs, including the proper configuration of your printer for the best results, preparing your images for printing by changing their orientation, and the printing process itself. I also demonstrated how you can select and print images directly from your camera's memory card by using the HP PhotoSmart inkjet printer.

In Chapter 6, I'll discuss the best way to store your rapidly-expanding collection of digital photographs.

→ # Storing Your Images

IN THIS CHAPTER
- Recording images to a CD-R or CD-RW disc
- Using Zip and SuperDisk drives
- Using Jaz and Orb drives

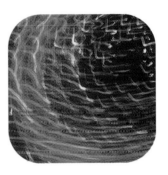

Let's face it — storing your masterpieces of digital photography on a floppy disk is less than smart. If you simply leave your collection on your computer, you're entrusting your priceless images to your hard drive, a piece of machinery that's been proven to be somewhat less than trustworthy. Kids, viruses, badly written software — any of them can cause the loss of your best work. What can you do? How can you store your collection permanently, or carry it with you while you're traveling without lugging around a laptop computer?

That's what this chapter is all about: Permanently safeguarding your images to protect them against disaster, and taking them with you on the road. I discuss several different types of storage, including CD-R and CD-RW discs, Zip and SuperDisk drives, removable hard drives, and Jaz and Orb drives. I also demonstrate how to write your images to a CD-R disc using the popular recording application Easy CD Creator from Adaptec.

Recording Images to a CD-R or CD-RW Disc

First, let's discuss *archival storage* for your finished images — consider this the ultimate backup for older images in your collection that have already been altered and edited. In the future, you'll simply want to access these images occasionally; for example, you might build a computer screensaver or add one of these images to a greeting card or a Word document.

Advantages of CD-R discs

The CD-R disc — that's short for "Compact Disc — Recordable" — is the perfect storage method for archiving your images. Why? Here's the list of the advantages of CD-R that any digital photographer will appreciate:

- **Foolproof storage.** A CD-R disc is practically the perfect backup media — with the proper care a CD-ROM will last for a century or more. (By that time, the human race will probably have

advanced far beyond the digital camera . . . but then, won't your descendents still want that photo of you and your bowling trophies?) Take my word for it — floppy disks are not a reliable, safe method of storing computer data, so don't trust them to hold anything that's valuable to you!

- **Plenty of space.** A CD-R disc can store anywhere from about 650 to 700MB of images. Even if you shoot your images without using your camera's compression feature, that amount of space can hold quite a collection.

- **They're fast.** You can retrieve your images from a CD-ROM in seconds (unlike a floppy disk, where you can practically read this entire chapter while your computer is loading images).

- **They're inexpensive.** CD-R drives for your computer start under $200 these days, and a spindle of 50 discs should cost you under $30. (I just saw an ad offering 100 for $14.99!)

- **They're universal.** A CD-R disc that you record yourself can be read in any computer with a CD-ROM drive — making it an ideal method of transporting your images from place to place.

Tip

Although this book covers just digital images, there are dozens of other reasons to buy a CD recorder — you can store any type of file (including MP3 audio and digital video) and even record your own audio CDs that you can play in your home or car CD player! I discuss all of these types of discs and how you can record them in my *Hewlett-Packard Official Recordable CD Handbook*, from Hungry Minds, Inc.

"Okay, Mark," you're saying, "what's the downside to a CD-R? There has got to be one." Sure enough, there is — you can only write information to a CD-R once, and it can only hold a maximum of 650 to 700MB. Unlike a hard drive, you can't erase a CD-R disc — but, if you remember the kids, that may be an advantage after all!

Before I explain how to record information to a disc, let's discuss the other type of recordable CD-ROM: the CD-RW.

Advantages of CD-RW discs

A CD-RW disc — short for "Compact Disc — Rewritable" — has all the same advantages as a CD-R disc, but it's more expensive (averaging about $5 each). Why the extra cost? Because a CD-RW disc can be erased and reused! You can format a CD-RW disc just as you do a hard drive (or, for that matter, your digital camera's memory card).

This technology has one downside, however: A CD-RW disc can't be read in older CD-ROM drives (unlike a CD-R, which any computer CD-ROM drive can read, no matter how old). Because today's CD recorders can create both CD-R and CD-RW discs, this really isn't too much of a problem. If you need to be able to erase the contents of a disc, use a CD-RW. If you need to be able to read a disc you've recorded on *any* CD-ROM drive (no matter how old it is), then use a CD-R disc.

Choosing a drive

Now, let's talk drives for a moment. In the PC world, a CD recorder can be either internal or external, while Mac CD-RW drives are usually external. If you decide on an external drive, you can choose either of two methods to connect it to your computer: USB and FireWire. USB, short for "Universal Serial Bus," is a popular interface for connecting all sorts of external devices, including digital cameras, to most PC and Macintosh computers. FireWire is an interface connection that shares most of the features of USB, although it's less common and transfers data much faster. External CD recorders that use FireWire connections offer much higher speeds than their USB counterparts, but FireWire drives are more expensive (and you need a FireWire port on your computer). This leaves me with two recommendations for most digital photographers who want to store their images on CD-R and CD-RW:

- **An internal CD-RW drive.** A good pick for most full-size desktop PC owners. Almost all PCs can use an internal drive with an IDE interface — if you have a SCSI adapter card and SCSI devices on your computer, you should also be able to connect an internal SCSI recorder.

- **A USB external CD recorder.** A good pick for Mac and laptop owners (as well as those who don't want to open their computer's case to install a drive).

Another criterion to watch closely is the speed of the drive, which is measured as a multiple of the speed of the original CD-ROM drives. The higher the "x" figure, the faster the drive will record. Most CD-RW drives use three figures in their specifications, and they normally refer to them in the form $10 \times 8 \times 32$, or something similar — the first number is the speed at which you can record CD-Rs, the second number is the speed at which you can record CD-RW discs, and the third number indicates the speed at which you can read a CD-ROM. (A CD recorder can also function as a simple CD-ROM read-only drive, like the drive that's usually included with just about every computer made these days.)

▲ Tip

A more expensive $10 \times$ CD recorder will offer faster recording speeds, but do you really need them? If you'll be recording only once a week as a backup, for example, you can save money by choosing a slower $4 \times$ drive. You may have to wait a bit longer for your disc, but you may also save $100 or more.

Choosing recording software

You can use dozens of different programs for recording — some are commercial programs, such as Adaptec's Easy CD Creator and CeQuadrat's WinOnCD, while others are shareware that you can download from the Internet, such as CDRWIN from Golden Hawk Technology.

Many of these programs are packed with technical features that help make the recording job easier, but there are really only two requirements for recording digital photographs:

- The recording software you choose must be able to create data CD-ROMs using files and folders from your hard drive.

- The software must be able to create discs using both the ISO and Microsoft Joliet data formats.

With these features, you can create the widest range of discs for PCs, the Macintosh and even Linux, ensuring that you can produce a recording that just about anyone can read, no matter what kind of strange hardware they're using!

Luckily, you probably won't have to buy this software for your CD-RW drive, because virtually every drive on the market comes bundled with one recording program or another. The most popular is probably Adaptec's Easy CD Creator — it's my favorite recording application. It's not called "easy" for nothing!

Recording images with Easy CD Creator

Let's run through the process of recording a folder's worth of digital photographs to a CD-R disc using Adaptec's Easy CD Creator. Here are the steps:

1. When you load a blank CD-R disc into your drive, the Create CD Wizard welcome screen (shown in Figure 6.1) automatically appears.

2. Click the Data button and click Data CD. Easy CD Creator loads and displays the Data CD Layout screen shown in Figure 6.2.

3. Use the Explorer pane at the top right of the Layout window to locate the digital photographs you want to record. To select a file or folder, click the icon to highlight it. To highlight multiple files and folders, hold down the Ctrl key while you click each icon.

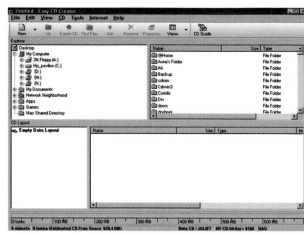

Figure 6.2 An empty Data CD layout, ready for you to add files and folders.

4. Click the Add button in the toolbar to copy the files, as shown in Figure 6.3.

▲ Tip

You can also add files and folders to your layout by clicking the selected icons and dragging them to the CD layout in the lower-left portion of the window. To drag an icon, hold down the mouse button while you move it.

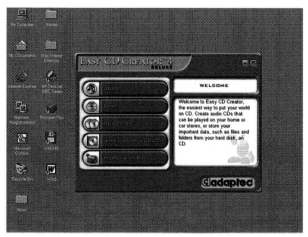

Figure 6.1 The Adaptec Easy CD Creator Create CD Wizard.

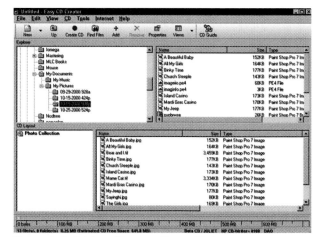

Figure 6.3 Adding files to a Data CD layout.

5. Repeat Steps 3 and 4 until all of your images have been added to the layout. You can add about 650MB to a standard CD-R disc. The bar at the bottom of the window marked in megabytes indicates approximately how much of the disc will be used by the files you add.

6. Click the Create CD button on the toolbar; the program displays the CD Creation Setup dialog box shown in Figure 6.4.

7. Click Advanced to display the advanced settings screen shown in Figure 6.5.

8. To test the recording process first, click Test and Create—if the test recording completes successfully, the program automatically records the disc afterwards.

9. To make multiple copies of your image collection, click the arrows next to the Number of Copies field to specify two or more copies.

10. Choose Track-at-once mode and select the Close the CD option, which permanently "write-protects" the CD so that it can't be written to again in the future.

11. To save these settings as the defaults for future recordings, click Set as Default.

12. Click OK to begin recording.

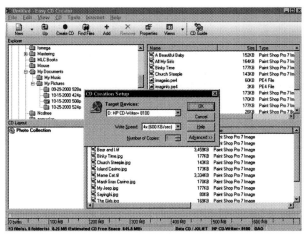

Figure 6.5 The advanced settings available within the CD Creation Setup dialog box.

Using Zip and SuperDisk Drives

If you'd rather not bother with recording a CD, you have other alternatives to storing your collection of digital photographs. For example, the Iomega Zip drive uses a cartridge that looks somewhat like a thick floppy disk, but it's much more reliable and much faster (about the speed of a CD-ROM drive). The first Zip drives held 100MB on a disk, while the latest version of the drive holds 250MB of data (which should be enough for just about any amateur photographer).

The Zip drive also doesn't need special recording software such as a CD recorder—you can write to it (and erase it) just as you would write to a regular floppy or a hard drive, using Windows Explorer or any program. The Zip drive is compatible with both Windows and MacOS.

The parallel port version of the Zip drive simply connects to your printer port. The Zip drive is also available in a SCSI version (which is much faster than its parallel port sibling, but requires a SCSI adapter card) and a USB version that works with the latest PCs and Macs.

The Imation SuperDisk drive is similar to the Zip drive in many ways, but it has one big

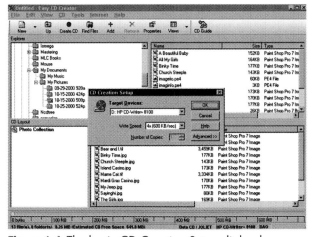

Figure 6.4 The basic CD Creation Setup dialog box.

advantage—it can also read and write to a standard floppy disk as well, making it a great choice for iMac and laptop owners. The SuperDisk drive can store 120MB on a single disk, and drives are available with parallel port, SCSI, and USB connections, as well as a PCMCIA version for laptop owners.

On the downside, however, a computer needs a Zip or SuperDisk drive to be able to read a cartridge—if you record those images to a CD, just about any computer around today can read it. Also, both types of removable disks are much more expensive than a CD-R or CD-RW disc, so collecting images on these disks can be expensive. Magnetic and tape media don't have the archival qualities of optical media, so if you want to ensure that your images are safe for a century, then a CD-ROM is the way to go. Finally, the size of these disks can result in a shelf full of plastic. With a collection of images on CD-ROM instead, you can store the entire library in the space of one or two computer books.

Using Jaz and Orb Drives

There's yet another possibility for storing your images—a removable cartridge hard drive system such as the Iomega Jaz drive, which can hold 2GB on a single cartridge. The Jaz cartridge actually contains a hard drive platter, so you can think of it as removing the "insides" of a hard drive when you eject it from the drive! However, these cartridges are designed to be carried with you, so they're as rugged as a four-wheel-drive Jeep, and 2GB is a tremendous amount of storage—that's more than three times the storage capacity of a CD-ROM. Again, no special recording program is needed to use a Jaz drive, so you won't be spending additional cash on software.

Jaz drives are much faster than either CD-ROMs or Zip/SuperDisk drives, too—as you might imagine, they're as fast as a regular internal hard drive. The internal Jaz drive for your desktop computer currently sells for about $300, while the external Jaz drive for a Mac or a laptop computer costs a bit more at $400. Cartridges usually cost about $120 each.

All is not perfect in the Jaz world, however; these drives require a SCSI connection, so you'll need to add a SCSI adapter to your computer. The external Jaz drive is also pretty hefty at two pounds, so it's a little less portable than a Zip or SuperDisk drive—you may find it hard to store in your laptop's case.

On the other hand, the Orb drive from Castlewood Systems offers similar capacity, rugged construction, and speed, but a much wider array of internal and external connections, including parallel port, USB, IDE, and SCSI. These drives are cheaper than the Jaz, too; you'll find Orb drives selling for about $200 for the internal versions and about $250 for the external models. Cartridges are cheaper, too—around $25 per cartridge.

Again, neither of these cartridges is anywhere near as universal as a CD-R disc, but if you're simply looking for a reliable backup for your digital photographs (and your other data files on your computer as well), these drives will work just fine. If you will be traveling with your images, consider an external model that connects to a parallel or USB port.

Summary

This chapter explored various methods of storing your collection of digital photographs—images written to a CD-R disc are permanent and can't be erased and reused, while images written to a CD-RW disc or a removable drive such as the Zip, Jaz, or Orb drives can be erased and updated as necessary. I discussed the pros and cons of each type of storage, including their cost, speed, and capacity. To demonstrate a typical session with a CD-RW drive, I also used Easy CD Creator to record a series of images from a folder to a CD-R disc.

Coming up next, Chapter 7 introduces you to lighting and exposure in digital photography.

Advanced Digital Photography Topics

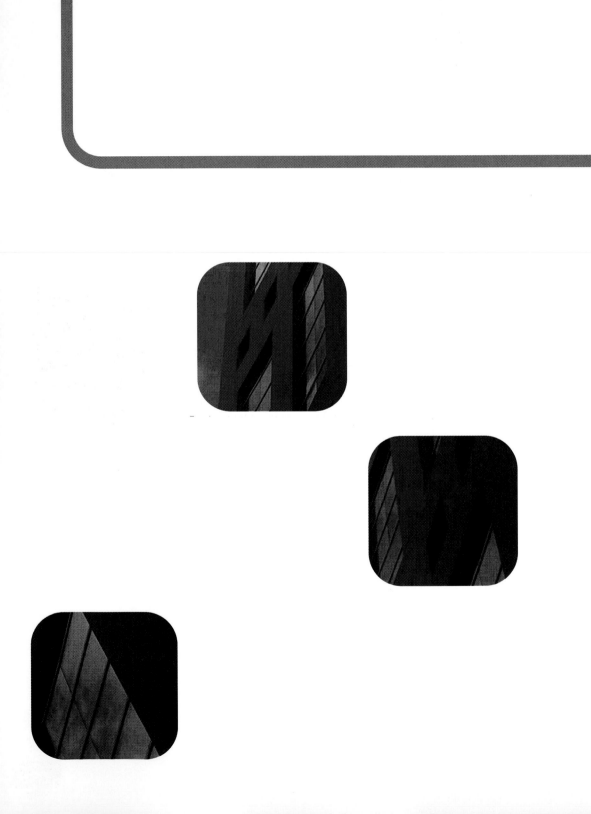

Light and Exposure Explained

IN THIS CHAPTER
- Using existing light
- Understanding color and white
- Judging exposure: Aperture and shutter speed
- Flash photography do's and don'ts

nyone who's taken his or her fair share of low-light photographs knows that there's more to lighting than a simple flashbulb! Film and digital cameras are very much alike in this regard, and handle exposure, aperture, and shutter speed in similar fashion — therefore, if you've had experience with the manual controls of a good 35mm camera, you'll feel right at home.

However, even if your digital camera is a fully automatic "point-and-shoot" model and offers no manual controls, don't skip this chapter — the tips and tricks I include here can help you take better pictures in differing light, with flash and without, no matter what type of camera you own.

Using Existing Light

First, let me present one of the cornerstones of good photography: Your subject may look better in *existing* light than enhanced lighting! To translate, many photographs that you take may appear to need a flash, but they'll actually look far better using only the natural lighting available from the subject and its surroundings.

By the way, this rule takes many photographers years to understand. (I'm included in that number.) Why? Simply because we got our start with automatic cameras that featured automatic flash — and although the camera does all the work, it has no sense of artistic lighting. These cameras have a rudimentary light meter that sets exposure and flash by very heavy-handed guidelines. It was only after I bought my first camera with manual controls that I learned to appreciate the existing light around a subject.

For example, consider the photograph in Figure 7.1 — how would this shot have looked if *any* type of flash had been used? To be honest, if a flash had been involved, there would probably have been no picture at all (unless you like window frames, that is). Notice that the image captures more than just the geometry of the scene and the outside light — without a flash, the *color* of the incoming light is captured as well! Unfortunately, a camera's flash often distorts the color of the existing light in a scene by "washing it out" in the glare of artificial illumination.

Figure 7.1 "Mission Dolores, San Francisco" — existing light at its finest! Photograph by Michael D. Welch.

With existing light, you can also preserve the poetry of light — the shadows on and around your subject. The shadows in the photograph shown in Figure 7.2 are a perfect illustration; with a flash, I would have lost all of the dramatic effect of the shadows cast by the staircase and the progression from dark to light. The image probably would have lost color as well.

Figure 7.2 "French Quarter Staircase," showing the shadows that result from existing lighting.

Keep these tips in mind when considering whether you should use existing light:

■ First, does your digital camera enable you to disable the flash entirely? If not, I would strongly recommend that you consider another camera, at least for shots involving existing light. Never completely trust your camera's flash system!

■ Is the subject illuminated from within, as the colorful sign in Figure 7.3? If so, it's usually better to use existing light and let the subject speak for itself, especially in low-light conditions. (After all, that's probably what a subject such as this was designed to do.)

Figure 7.4 "Time Tunnel," taken using existing light.

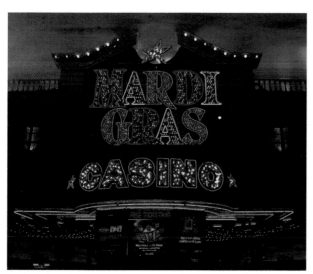

Figure 7.3 "Casino." The illumination from this sign speaks for itself.

■ Is there a sharp line of light and shadow, as in my shot in Figure 7.4? This home in New Orleans dates back to 1910, and this long hallway is unlit — the "tunnel" effect and the explosion of light and color at the end would have been ruined by a flash, as you can see in Figure 7.5.

■ If you think that a subject might look better in existing light, by all means experiment! Take one shot with existing light as well as a shot with flash; I do this on a regular basis.

■ It's especially important to hold your camera steady during shots taken with no flash, because your camera may calculate a longer exposure time! If you have the time and your tripod is handy, you should definitely use it to avoid a blurry image.

■ Windows are a photographer's joy! (Unless you have to shoot through or into one, that is.) They're perfect for creating a play of light and shadow with just about any subject, and they offer natural lighting. If the window has curtains, use them in case of direct sunlight.

Figure 7.5 Using a flash, the effect of the previous shot is lost.

Understanding Color and White

Of course, I know you're aware of the simple difference between color and white, but in the world of digital photography there's more to discuss — your camera is sensitive to light in different ways than the human eye.

To begin, all so-called "white" light is *not* created equal. You may have noticed that there's a difference between the light produced by a typical light bulb, a fluorescent lamp, a halogen bulb, and the sun — if you spend your time perched in front of a computer monitor as much as I do, of course, you may not see natural sunlight as often! Here are two examples:

- If you've bought cosmetics before, you may have encountered a makeup mirror that could be set to match different types of light; a shade of lipstick might look different in an office environment, where fluorescent lights are used, than it does outside.

- Both Windows and MacOS have built-in color matching systems for all sorts of display and print devices. These systems let you adjust the hue and brightness of the white and the colors you see onscreen so that they more closely duplicate the colors produced by your printer. Graphic artists, painters and color-savvy photographers often refer to the specific hue of a color as its *temperature* (the scale is actually based on heat, measured in degrees Kelvin).

Film photographers can use different types of lens filters to compensate for the color differences in different lighting — it's a hassle, but it's the only way to ensure accurate color when you're using film. Digital photographers, on the other hand, have additional methods, depending on the camera, of solving problems with changing lighting:

- **Automatic and manual white balancing.** Virtually all digital cameras automatically adjust the white component of incoming light to "absolute" white, so that changes in lighting won't affect the colors you see in the final image. That's all that most of us need, but more expensive cameras can give you manual control over the white balance in your photographs, which is useful for special effects and extreme lighting conditions. (Remember the red light you always see as illumination in submarine movies? That helps the crew maintain its night vision.)

- **Built-in electronic filters.** Some digital cameras have manual filters and color balancing programmed into their operating system to help you compensate for different lighting conditions. You can adjust for Tungsten (indoor lamp light), Fluorescent (office lighting), Daylight, and Flash. These settings are typically accessed and set through an LCD menu on the camera. You can even choose Black & White or Sepia tone to add a more artistic look to your photographs.

■ **Your friendly image editor.** You can completely alter the hue and saturation of the colors in your digital photographs by using an image editor, such as Photoshop.

Judging Exposure: Aperture and Shutter Speed

Our next stop in the digital world of light takes us to aperture and shutter speed. To refresh your memory:

■ The *aperture* of a camera determines how much light enters the camera through the shutter, and it's typically measured in f-stops — the smaller the f-stop number, the more light is admitted.

■ The *shutter speed* of a camera is the amount of time the shutter remains open to admit light.

Together, these two settings control the *exposure*: the total amount of light that the sensors at the back of the camera receive and the length of time that light enters the camera. Exposure is handled on today's digital cameras in three ways:

■ **Totally automatic.** Just as it sounds — you have no control over either aperture or shutter speed. With a camera like this, you can basically skip the rest of this section.

■ **Manual aperture or shutter.** In this mode, you select the aperture (or shutter speed), and the camera automatically selects the best shutter speed (or aperture) to match.

■ **Totally manual.** You can completely control both aperture and shutter speed.

Overriding the automatic exposure feature is usually a simple procedure — for example, you use the photo LCD screen on the HP PhotoSmart C200 camera, selecting an exposure level using the arrow buttons on the back. If you like, you can think of adjustments such as these as "bumping" the exposure up or down for a particularly dark room or a

shot in bright sunlight. However, unlike overriding the flash setting, I generally don't set exposure manually. (If you prefer to think of your digital camera's circuitry as an electronic "brain," the lobe that controls exposure is usually much better at estimating things.)

If you'd like to experiment with exposure, these guidelines may help:

■ If your camera does offer manual exposure but doesn't feature an onboard exposure meter that you can use, you need to buy a handheld meter at a local photo shop. Without an exposure meter, you're basically walking blindfolded, because the human eye is notoriously bad at gauging light. (I recommend a handheld model that can perform both spot and averaged metering, so it can be used under the widest range of conditions.)

■ It's always a better idea to underexpose an image than overexpose it — you can always turn to your trusty image editor to lighten things up, but it's practically impossible to darken a digital photograph and produce something you'd want to keep.

■ Aim your exposure meter to check the subject, not the overall scene — this is especially important if there's a high contrast between subject and background. Without a focus on the subject, the reading will tend to overexpose a dark subject and underexpose a bright one.

■ Unsure about an exact exposure? Of course, this is less of a problem with a digital camera, where you can usually see the results immediately, but what if you're shooting in bright sunlight, and you can't see the results on the LCD screen? Or, perhaps you can't adjust your LCD screen, and it consistently shows images too light or dark. In cases like this, you can use an old film photography trick called *bracketing*: After you've taken a shot at what you think is the correct exposure, take one or two images with the exposure set somewhat under and one or two images somewhat over the original exposure. (This trick works with both manual aperture and manual shutter cameras, although the camera does part of the work automatically.) For example, if you have a manual shutter model and your first exposure was taken at 1/30, try bracketing with two shots at 1/15 and 1/60. For a manual aperture camera and a first exposure at f-4, try f-2.8 and f-5.6. Because you can usually delete the images that don't work later and regain that space for more shots, bracketing makes even better sense when you're using a digital camera. Some cameras (such as the HP PhotoSmart 912) offer a bracketing function that automatically shoots several shots at different exposures.

Flash Photography Do's and Don'ts

Earlier in the chapter, I discussed the joys of existing light, but don't get me wrong — your camera's flash, when properly used, can deliver photographs you'd never get with existing light. This includes, by the way, images that you take in bright sunlight, where most novice photographers feel that no flash is required. For example, look at the demonstration in Figures 7.6 and 7.7; without the extra flash to "fill" the subject, we lose her face because of the shadow from the hat.

Tip

In a situation where the subject is backlit, it's a very good idea to force your camera's flash on — otherwise, the camera may judge the scene to be so bright that it doesn't warrant a flash.

I've already spoken in Chapter 2 about the different flash modes you'll find on most cameras, so I won't go into what's available on most cameras now. Here's the good news: No matter what controls your camera offers for its flash system (including none at all), the same rules apply. Here's a detailed list of flash "Do's and Don'ts" that you can follow:

- **Don't** place the subject right in front of a reflective surface, such as a painted wall — this gives you the classic "mug shot" shadow, which I avoid like the plague. Instead, move the subject a couple of feet in front of the wall, and you'll lose both the shadow and the possibility of an overexposure due to that reflected flash.

- **Do** use your flash to compensate for light shining behind the subject — for instance, a tree that's in shadow with bright sunlight behind it. (This is often called *backlighting*.) Like the example in Figure 7.7, the "fill" flash helps even out the surface detail on the subject, which would otherwise be in shadow or turn out as a silhouette.

Figure 7.6 Outdoor snapshot taken without a flash.

Figure 7.7 The same image, improved with the use of a flash.

- **Don't** shoot through a sheet of glass or plastic with a flash — you'll likely set up a reflection or "hot spot" that will spoil the image. If the subject has adequate lighting behind the surface, try turning off your flash and using existing light or use an auxiliary light source (more on this in a second). If you're shooting a portrait of a person wearing glasses, try to take the image slightly to one side; the off-center angle will help cut down on reflections. Learn to be careful around other highly reflective surfaces, such as polished wood or metal, too.

- **Do** use an auxiliary light source as a *bounce* flash — so-called because it can be pointed toward a wall or ceiling to "bounce" indirect light on the subject. This is a good trick to use for reflective surfaces, to add more light to a room that would otherwise be too dark using a single flash, or to avoid a harsh glare of a fixed flash on a subject. You can find a bounce flash for your camera at a photo shop, or you can even make do with a simple desk lamp that can be adjusted and aimed where you need it. Figure 7.8 is a good example of bounce lighting at work — this enclosed doorway is normally dark at all times of the day, but with a secondary lamp aimed at the top of the entrance I was able to even out the lighting. In this case, the lamp was a powerful flashlight that I covered with a sheet of semi-transparent white plastic.

- **Do** make sure that your subject is evenly illuminated by your flash — a simple example is a long wall with paintings, where shooting from one end of the wall leaves the other end in near-darkness. Again, if you have to, use an auxiliary light source placed off-camera.

- **Do** experiment with colored filters on your auxiliary lighting — or, if you can safely tape a strip of colored plastic over your camera's flash without affecting the lens, you can create a neat effect. (You can also recreate this effect with an image editor, but is that as much fun?)

Figure 7.8 The indirect light from an auxiliary source helps illuminate a dark entranceway.

- **Do** add auxiliary lighting for extreme close-up photography. Unless the subject is giving off light itself or you're shooting in bright sunlight, existing light is almost never enough to highlight details and provide complete illumination in close-ups (no matter what exposure settings you choose). It's usually not a good idea to use your camera's flash to illuminate macro shots, which may overwhelm the image, depending on your flash range and its ability to adjust.

Summary

We covered a lot of tips and tricks in this chapter, and they included a range of subjects dealing with lighting, exposure, and flash photography. You learned how exposure is controlled by a digital camera, and I outlined guidelines for shooting photographs by using your camera's manual exposure controls. Finally, I discussed several different uses for your flash and how to avoid common problems that result from flash photography.

In Chapter 8, the word is "optics" as we discuss lenses in detail.

→ # Your Lens Is Your Friend!

IN THIS CHAPTER
- A quick tour of different lenses
- Comparing optical and digital zoom
- Controlling focal length
- Estimating depth of field
- Autofocus mysteries revealed

The carpenter, the plumber, and the mechanic have their toolboxes. Serious photographers typically have a collection of lenses in their camera bag as well. Sure, lenses are tools . . . although you can't drive a nail with a telephoto lens (try attaching a hammer to your camera!).

If you've chosen a digital camera that can accept external lenses, you've opened your creative horizons — and this chapter helps you chart a course through them. You'll learn what special-purpose lenses you can add and the effects they'll have on your digital photographs.

Don't worry, however, if your camera is a fixed-lens model without an external mount or adapter — there's still plenty of information in this chapter concerning zoom and autofocus, as well as discussions of focal length and depth of field.

A Quick Tour of Different Lenses

If you've spent less than $500 or so on your digital camera, it probably features a "one-size-fits-all" fixed-focus primary lens. This standard lens is appropriate for subjects at a distance of anywhere from a foot and a half away to "infinity" (you have to be a little forgiving of the term, because it really means the visible horizon) — perfect for the type of snapshots that form the basis for family photo albums around the world.

But what if your subject is far away, and it's difficult to capture detail or fill the frame with your subject? Or perhaps you're taking a scenic shot, and you'd like to capture as much as possible of the breathtaking view in a single image? Now you're entering the realm of specialized lenses that can perform tasks beyond the capabilities of a standard camera. In this section, I'll discuss each of the specialized lenses that can be fitted on a digital camera.

The telephoto lens

The most widely-known of the photographer's accessory lenses is the *telephoto* lens — it immediately conjures up images of spies, such as James

Bond, and police work. Even if you're not a secret agent, however, you'll find a telephoto useful for other purposes:

- **Wildlife photographs.** A telephoto enables you to photograph animals that you could never approach close enough with a standard camera lens (either because they or you would be too easily frightened). With a telephoto lens, you can keep your distance and avoid scaring the animals with all that humming and clicking.

- **Sports shots.** Stuck halfway up the stadium or across the field from the action? A telephoto lens makes it easier to snap a photo of your favorite player.

- **Architectural photos.** With a telephoto lens, you can photograph building details from the ground or across the street.

Remember the term *focal length* that I discussed in Chapter 2? The telephoto lens works its magic with a longer focal length than a standard lens, which, as a tradeoff, means that it has a smaller *field of view,* which is the area of the scene taken in by the lens (measured in degrees). Therefore, photographs that you take with a telephoto lens capture less of the scene than a standard lens. (Luckily, this isn't usually a problem because your subject is usually dominant in photographs taken by using a telephoto lens.)

The macro lens

On the other end of the spectrum, the *macro lens* is the photographer's pick for extreme close-up shots, such as the one you see in Figure 8.1. Macro lenses can focus to mere inches in front of the camera (and, in a pinch, you can even adjust them to act as a standard lens). Because of the exceptional detail that these lenses deliver with smaller objects, macro lenses are popular picks for professional photographers that take "product shots" for manufacturing companies or hobbyists, such as coin and stamp collectors.

Many digital cameras can actually produce the same type of extreme close up by using a *macro mode.* Some high-end models have a secondary macro lens in addition to their standard lens. Others adjust their internal lenses and focusing for macro shots — for example, the HP PhotoSmart 210 and 215 cameras let you to get as close as 1½ inches away from your subject. Be sure to use the camera's LCD screen to view and properly frame your macro shots, but keep in mind that automatic focusing does not occur until the shutter button is pressed halfway down. Your image on the LCD may appear fuzzy or blurred until you do this.

Figure 8.1 Western fence lizard — an example of a macro lens close up. Photograph by Michael D. Welch.

The wide-angle lens

A wide-angle lens is the exact opposite of a telephoto lens; it features a shorter focal length and a larger field of view. A wide-angle lens is perfect for capturing the panorama of a scenic view — as you might expect, detail is lost in the bargain.

To illustrate, let's suppose that you're taking a photo of a soccer field from the stands. With a standard lens, you might only see a quarter of the field in one photo, but the players would be easier to see. On the other hand, a wide-angle lens would be able to capture much more of the entire field, but the players would shrink accordingly. (As my math teacher used to say in high school, "You can't have it both ways.")

Figure 8.2 was taken with a wide-angle lens; what better subject than a city skyline?

Figure 8.2 "Chicago Skyscape" — a wide-angle lens pulls in more of the scene.

The fish-eye lens

Let's return to our soccer field example. A wide-angle lens might be able to fit most of that scene into one photo, but it's not likely to accept the *entire* length of the field. You may be asking, "Hey, wait a second — I've seen panoramic photos that did just that! How do they take shots with such a wide angle?"

The secret is a special breed of wide-angle lens called a *fish-eye* lens. Yes, it actually bulges in front, just like its namesake, but don't mind the looks: One of these expensive lenses can photograph with a field of view from 140 to 180 degrees! Because the human eye can't actually match that huge degree of view, one of these photographs can display images that you and I could never take in ourselves.

There's a downside, though: To accept such a large view, a fish-eye lens distorts the edges of the photograph so they appear to "curve" toward the center (which remains in focus and distortion-free).

Silhouette and colored filters

Before I move to the next section, I'd like to briefly mention two popular types of filters used by film photographers:

- **Silhouettes.** These filters act much like a mask — they're simply pieces of black card stock or plastic that block part of the edges of an image. Silhouettes are typically used with portrait photos. For example, a silhouette might create a starburst or a diamond shape around a person's face.

- **Colors.** Colored filters can be used in two ways: to correct the color balance of a scene (due to the lighting) and to add special effects by turning all colors in an image to a single shade.

As a digital photographer, however, you'll probably use a silhouette or a filter rarely, if ever — chalk up another victory for image editing applications! You can add a border around your image by using just about any color or pattern, and reducing an image to a single color (or even transforming a color image to black-and-white) requires only a click or two of your mouse.

Comparing Optical and Digital Zoom

I mentioned optical and digital zoom way back in Chapter 2, but Figures 8.3 and 8.4 tell the tale: The photo taken with a true optical zoom, shown in Figure 8.3, delivers more detail and a clearer image than the digital zoom of the same magnification shown in Figure 8.4.

Figure 8.3 An optical zoom.

Figure 8.4 The same picture taken with a digital zoom.

Why the difference? With an optical zoom, the camera varies the focal length of the lens. A digital zoom merely resizes the center of the image (which it assumes to be the subject), using the same mathematic algorithm that an image editor might use — imagine stretching a sheet of rubber, and you can probably visualize what's happening. Personally, I use my camera's digital zoom feature only when I want to quickly crop the outside of a photograph and can't do it by moving closer to the subject or using optical zoom.

Although I prefer an optical zoom, it does have three drawbacks:

- **Low-light problems.** While a digital zoom is unaffected by the amount of light — after all, it's simply enlarging the subject — it's practically impossible to capture a clear and sharp image in a low-light scene. (This is why you see so few zoom photographs taken at dusk.)

- **Focus problems.** Because an optical zoom adjusts the focal length of the lens, objects in the scene that are not the same distance from the lens as your main subject — for example, a street sign in front of the building you're taking a picture of — quickly move out of focus as you zoom in.

- **Movement problems.** As you magnify the subject, you also magnify any motion you make while holding the camera. Again, a tripod can help ensure your camera is as stable as possible while taking photographs by using optical zoom.

> **Tip**
>
> Because taking a photograph by using your camera's optical zoom can be a tricky proposition if you're too close or too far from the subject, this is yet another good time to review a shot by using your camera's LCD screen as soon as you snap it. The results from that first exposure can help you determine if everything went right — and, if not, you can diagnose the problem and try again.

If your digital camera didn't come equipped with an optical zoom but it does have a lens mount or adapter, then you're in luck! You can invest in external zoom or telephoto lenses that will achieve the same results.

Controlling Focal Length

Now that you know more about focal length, keep in mind that you have three different ways to control the size of your subject on today's digital cameras:

- **Fixed focal length.** This is the most common method — no control at all! If the lens is interchangeable but has a fixed focal length, you'll have to swap it with another lens that has a different length to change the size of your subject. (Alternately, you can simply move toward the subject to enlarge it, or back to reduce it — the "human zoom.")

- **Zoom.** As I covered in the previous section, you can alter the focal length of an optical zoom lens to enlarge the subject — no swapping lenses, and no trudging closer to your subject. More expensive cameras carry built-in zoom lenses, while others can be mounted externally.

- **An auxiliary lens.** Finally, you can add an auxiliary lens to the front of your camera's existing lens — this is rather like a person with weak eyesight putting on a pair of reading glasses. Auxiliary lenses are available for both standard lenses and telephoto lenses; if you've seen a digital or film camera with an outrageously-long barrel, it's likely to be using both a telephoto and an auxiliary lens. (Perhaps that photographer was shooting Alaskan bald eagles in their nests from hundreds of feet away.)

Which method you use depends on the existing lens system in your camera and whether your camera body has an external lens mount. (If you're on a holiday trip and you have only your point-and-shoot automatic with a fixed focal length with you, it's time to use your feet to "change" focal length.)

Estimating Depth of Field

If your digital camera doesn't enable you to adjust the focal length of your image, you're liable to see a number of images with the subject in clear focus and the background almost unrecognizable.

Figure 8.5 illustrates this effect (which can also occur with both telephoto and macro lenses), using the HP PhotoSmart 912 digital camera as a subject; note how the camera's image is crisp and sharp, while the base of the lamp and the picture frame are completely out of focus.

Figure 8.5 Depending on the depth of field, a sharply focused subject may appear with background objects that are out of focus.

If you can manually set the lens characteristics on your camera, however, it is possible to estimate the distance range where objects are in sharp focus. To do this, use a *depth of field scale*.

If you use a digital camera that accepts external lenses, they may carry a separate depth of field scale on the outside of the lens. (Alternately, your local photo shop can probably sell you a hand-held electronic depth of field scale that can be adjusted for different lenses.) Using the scale, you can estimate the proper f-stop setting and the distance range that will be in focus.

With this information in hand, it's easy to compose images with everything in sharp focus by setting up your camera at the proper distance — or, if you'd like to be creative, you can predict which objects in the scene will be in focus and which will not.

Autofocus Mysteries Revealed

Today's digital cameras have several levels of manual focusing control. Depending on the money you've spent, you'll encounter everything from fixed focus and fully automatic (with no manual settings) to the traditional fully manual focusing you'd find on a 35mm SLR film camera. Naturally, autofocus is by far the most popular system.

Because every camera handles focusing differently (and with a unique set of buttons, menus, and rotary controls to boot), I won't be covering the basics of focusing your digital camera in this section; I'll refer you to your camera's instruction manual for that. (If focusing isn't covered in your instruction manual, then I would recommend a suitable letter be sent to the manufacturer!) However, I can provide you with the autofocusing tips and tricks that your camera's manual may not include.

- **An image editor can't fix an out-of-focus shot!** I'll take this opportunity to correct a common myth among Candid Snapshooters: no matter how rare the scene or how good the subject, it's practically impossible to correct a badly focused shot with your image editor. Digital photography is actually the same as film photography in this regard — you must focus your shot correctly, whether it's exposed on film or saved as binary data.

- **Know the limitations of your autofocus system.** Digital cameras typically use either a *passive or active infrared sensor* for focusing (which works

better at nighttime and with low levels of existing light) or *CCD focusing* (which does rapid previews of the scene at different settings until edges of objects in the scene appear sharp to the sensor). Some cameras use a combination of these two methods. Find out what the range of your autofocus system is, and take your photographs within this range. Also, it's a good idea to check your camera's manual to determine its minimum focusing distance.

▲ **Tip**

Keep in mind that most autofocus cameras focus on the *center* of the image frame, so if your subject is at the corner of the frame the scene may "fool" your camera — take a first exposure and check it with your LCD screen to see how it came out. You may need to bring your subject closer to the center of the frame for correct focusing.

- **Use a focus/infinity lock.** If your camera has a *focus lock* (also called an infinity lock), you can use it to force your camera to focus to a certain distance. For example, you can set your camera to ignore other objects that may be in front of the main subject and focus on a certain distance, or you can set your camera to ignore a glass windowpane and focus instead on the horizon.

- **Remember the pause!** An autofocus camera requires a second or two to determine the distance to the subject and focus the image — this can be yet another stumbling block in taking good photographs of a subject in motion with a digital camera. Whenever possible, focus beforehand on an object that will be at the same distance, or use your focus lock.

- **Check your focus by using the LCD screen.** Although that LCD screen eats battery power, it's a great tool for judging the effect of a manual focus. Also, an LCD screen doesn't suffer from *parallax* when taking close ups — a term that refers to the discrepancy between your optical viewfinder and your camera's lens at short focusing ranges (caused by the distance between the viewfinder's window and the lens). If you're running low on battery power and you have to use your optical viewfinder for a close-up shot, use the border markings in the viewfinder to account for the parallax. Your camera's manual should specify the range where parallax can occur and how to use the alternate framing provided by the viewfinder's border markings.

Summary

In this chapter, you learned all about the wide, wonderful world of lenses — from the fixed and autofocus lenses common on low- to medium-priced digital cameras to the fully manual focus lenses on more expensive models. I also introduced you to the special auxiliary lenses available for cameras with lens mounts, such as telephoto, wide-angle, and macro lenses. I also provided tips and tricks for gauging and controlling depth of field and focal length with both your camera's standard lens and external lenses. Finally, I discussed autofocusing and guidelines you can use to help accurately focus photographs at any range.

Chapter 9 covers photo composition, previewing, and photo management.

Understanding Photo Composition

IN THIS CHAPTER
- Can't I just point and shoot?
- Rules of composition
- Composition do's and don'ts
- Reviewing the shot
- Deleting images from the camera
- Correcting composition — after the shot

What makes the difference between a Candid Snapshooter and a serious photographer? In Chapter 2, I pointed out differences in equipment and features that help your creative side and make things easier, but, in all honesty, the amount of money that you've spent on your equipment and the number of lenses in your camera bag won't guarantee a better photograph. Great photographs are taken every day by folks with fixed-focus, "point-and-shoot" automatic cameras, while others who have spent thousands on their digital cameras take the same old snapshots in the time-honored tradition. Don't get me wrong . . . there's certainly nothing wrong with taking snapshots, but they won't make you a serious photographer!

If you're satisfied with snapshots, go ahead and skip to the next chapter—but if you'd like to take better photographs, stick around! In this chapter, I discuss what really sets a serious photographer apart from the rest: composition, or the art of building a scene or capturing a vision *before* you press the shutter release.

Figure 9.1 A simple snapshot.

Can't I Just Point and Shoot?

Put simply, yes—you can just point and shoot! The rules that I'll be discussing in the following sections work just as well with a fully automatic camera as they do with the most expensive digital camera. Once you've learned the basics of good composition, you can apply them in a heartbeat to just about any photograph.

And that's the difference between the two images you see in Figures 9.1 and 9.2; the first is a basic snapshot, and the second is the same snapshot with the basic rules of composition applied. Both photos show the same subject, but I think you'll agree that the second image looks significantly better. There was no extra "setup" time required—I simply asked the girls to arrange themselves slightly differently, and the rest of the improvements were made by holding the camera differently and choosing better lighting.

Of course, sometimes you just don't have the luxury of arranging anything—and at those times, you take the photograph you can get. The rest of

Figure 9.2 The same snapshot improved by using basic composition techniques.

your shots, however, will benefit from some level of composition.

Rules of Composition

Different people have differing tastes in art—and, as you might expect, there's no one single set of composition rules for the "perfect" photograph. This section outlines the two popular guidelines for composing photographs. Each of them works in different situations. Try both, and use them to take better shots!

The Rule of Thirds

Probably the best-known rule of composition—and it applies to a variety of visual art, by the way, including painting and sculpture—is the "Rule of Thirds." It's very simple: divide the image frame into nine individual areas, as shown in Figure 9.3. The four lines dividing the areas and the intersections form the keys to this rule.

To follow this rule, your subject should be aligned along either:

- one of the four lines that cross the image

- one of the intersections

Naturally, if you have two or more subjects, they should also be aligned along one of these lines or intersections. Movement should also flow along these lines or stop at an intersection, if possible.

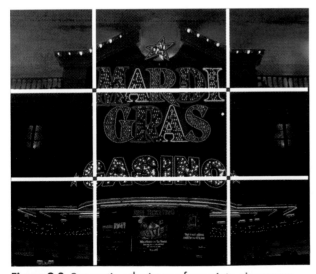

Figure 9.3 Separating the image frame into nine areas.

Once you're familiar with the Rule of Thirds, you'll notice that most professional photographs you see in books and magazines follow its lead. To illustrate, compare the images shown in Figure 9.4 and 9.5—the first shot simply centers the image in the frame, while the second image follows the Rule of Thirds. Although I think that both are good architectural photographs, which one do you find more visually interesting?

The Rule of Thirds applies to most of the images you'll take, but it's less useful with portrait and close-up photography.

The Rule of Asymmetry

Our second school of photo composition, the "Rule of Asymmetry," revolves around an asymmetrical relationship between the major subject and either one or more minor subjects or the background itself. The rule is to combine the three basic shapes—the square (or rectangle), the circle, and

Figure 9.4 "Aspire" — a church tower centered in the frame.

Figure 9.5 "On Columbus Avenue in San Francisco," which follows the Rule of Thirds. Photograph by Michael D. Welch.

Figure 9.7 "Cultures," an asymmetrical combination of basic shapes.

the triangle—to create a new contour shape. Also, the Rule of Asymmetry often includes a sharp contrast between lighter and darker elements in the scene, which also applies to bold patterns and shadow.

Figure 9.6 is a great example of an asymmetrical composition. Notice how the truck is essentially in the middle of the frame, but the barn provides a strong background shape with a solid color that contrasts sharply with the pattern. Together, they merge to form a new outline—in this school of composition, the major subject doesn't necessarily dominate the frame.

Unlike the Rule of Thirds, the subject(s) in an asymmetrical photograph can appear in any area within the frame—making it a good choice for a "still life," like my composition in Figure 9.7, or a portrait.

Composition Do's and Don'ts

No matter which rule of composition you're following, a number of well-known do's and don'ts will apply to your photographs—they can help turn a good picture into a great one. Ready? Here we go:

- **Do** try different camera angles. There's nothing wrong with a typical head-on treatment of the subject, but some of your best work results when you approach your scene from another angle.

- **Do** look for framing elements you can add to your scene. As an example, the arch of a building or a bridge (like the shot shown in Figure 9.8) helps focus attention on the subject and adds visual interest.

Figure 9.6 "Lemos Farm, Half Moon Bay, California" an asymmetrical composition. Photograph by Michael D. Welch.

Figure 9.8 "Mt. Baker from La Conner, Washington" uses a bridge to frame the subject. Photograph by Michael D. Welch.

- **Don't** place people in static poses. Whenever possible, use elements of the scene to add interest—a portrait subject could hold something, or sit at the base of a statue, or even be studying a book or another photograph.

- **Do** fill most of the frame with your subject. It's usually a good idea to draw close to your subject—you'll maximize the detail in your photograph. Of course, there are exceptions with scenic shots and multiple subjects, but for most photos, you'll want to stress the subject.

- **Don't** be afraid to change the orientation of your frame. Compare the images in Figures 9.9 and

9.10—by changing the orientation of the image, I avoided cutting the subject in half. You can also emphasize subjects with strong vertical lines using this trick.

- **Don't** place your subject in front of an awkward background object. Although that tree trunk or lamp post may seem like the ideal backdrop for a portrait, the final effect is a trunk or post "embedded" in your subject's head!

- **Do** point subjects and motion toward the center. This is a general rule—you usually don't want to show your subject from the rear, although I have seen exceptions!

Figure 9.10 By changing the orientation, the image includes more of the subject.

Figure 9.9 With the wrong orientation, the subject is chopped at the waist.

Figure 9.11 "New Westminster Leaves" focuses on the texture and color of the leaves rather than a specific subject. Photograph by Michael D. Welch.

- **Do** look for interesting shadows that can add visual impact — as I mentioned earlier in the book, you can use the shadows thrown by existing light or use an auxiliary light to provide your own shadows.

- **Do** keep an eye out for interesting textures — sometimes the texture can become the subject of the image all by itself! For example, the texture and colors in Figure 9.11 speak for themselves.

Reviewing the Shot

As I've mentioned often in earlier chapters, it's a good idea to review an important digital photograph as soon as you take it — if your camera has an LCD screen, you should be able to view the image you've just saved or view all of the images stored in your memory card. Some cameras even enable you to view your images on a TV screen with a direct hookup to the camera!

As an example, here are the steps you'd follow to review your images on an HP PhotoSmart C200 digital camera:

1. Close the lens cover to turn the camera off.

2. Press the LCD On/Off button to turn on the Photo LCD screen.

3. Press the left- or right-arrow button to cycle through your images.

4. Press the LCD On/Off button to turn off the Photo LCD screen when you're done.

Deleting Images from the Camera

Here's the situation: You're away from your computer and you can't download your images. Your memory card is completely full, and you didn't bring any spares. However, there's a once-in-a-lifetime view outside your window! So how do you take one or two extra photographs? If your camera has an image management system that enables you to delete images, you can view the photographs stored on your memory card and delete one or two shots to make room.

As an example, here are the steps you'd follow to delete one or more images from an HP PhotoSmart C200 digital camera:

1. Close the lens cover to turn the camera off.

2. Press the LCD On/Off button to turn on the Photo LCD screen.

3. Press the Menu button to display the image management menu on the Photo LCD screen.

4. Press the left- or right-arrow button to cycle through the choices on the menu until you've selected Erase.

5. Press the OK button to select the Erase function.

6. Press the left- or right-arrow button to cycle through the Erase menu. To erase all images, choose All. To erase the current image displayed in the background, choose One. To cancel the Erase function, choose None.

7. Press the OK button to complete the Erase function.

8. Press the LCD On/Off button to turn off the Photo LCD screen.

Correcting Composition — After the Shot

Before I close this chapter, I'd like to introduce you to three common procedures you can take to help correct composition mistakes. I'll be showing you how to take care of these problems later in the book, but I think it's a good idea to familiarize you with the "repairs" so you'll know which images can benefit from them.

Cropping

Cropping an image removes a specified section of a photograph — or the entire border — enabling you to remove extraneous objects in the background or at the edges of the shot. Most image-editing programs handle cropping in the same manner — you use your mouse to draw a box around the portion of the image you want to keep, and the rest of the image outside of the box is deleted.

Rotation

Next, you can rotate an image by any number of degrees to correct problems with alignment of the image with the frame. You won't need this procedure often; it really comes in handy, however, if you took a great photo in a hurry and were holding the camera slightly askew. As an example, say you took a fabulous sunset shot from a boat, but noticed after the sun went down that the horizon line was crooked. A small amount of rotation and perhaps a bit of cropping (to also straighten the photo's edges) will straighten that horizon.

▲ Tip

You can also use the rotation feature to change the orientation of an image as it was downloaded from your camera — use a 90 degree rotation, and you can turn the picture to face the correct way.

Resizing

I've already discussed the digital zoom feature offered by many digital cameras earlier in the book. Used judiciously in tandem with cropping, you can isolate and enlarge the subject of a photograph to fill more of the frame. (This can help if you couldn't get closer to your subject and didn't have a telephoto lens.) However, it's *very* easy to lose detail in your image when resizing, so it's best to experiment and save your results under a different file name until you've achieved the desired enlargement. For this reason, I use this technique only as a last resort.

Summary

Our subjects in this chapter were photo composition and image management — you learned about two popular rules that digital photographers use to compose better images, as well as solutions for composition problems that you can apply after the image has been downloaded to your computer. I also demonstrated how to use your camera's LCD screen and menu system to review an image after you take it and how to delete images from your Memory card.

In Chapter 10, I explain the details behind the various popular image formats in use today and show you how to convert photographs from one format to another.

File Formats Explained

IN THIS CHAPTER
- An introduction to popular file formats
- Converting images
- The importance of compression
- Preparing pictures

Unlike film photography, your digital images are not stored as negatives—instead, they're saved as files containing binary data on your computer. The image format you use to store your photographs determines a number of important characteristics, including how large the files are, how many colors they use, and what other computer programs can read them. Therefore, you should be familiar with formats and how to convert your image into another format whenever necessary.

Earlier in the book, I mentioned one or two popular image formats—but in this chapter I provide all the details and explain which formats are best for different applications (such as e-mail attachments and Web pages).

An Introduction to Popular File Formats

If you're familiar with PostScript, the language that many computers send to their printers to produce documents, you probably know that it's actually made up of English programming commands. That's not the case with the data stored in image files, however—an image format is just plain gibberish. So what separates one image file format from another? In this section, I weigh the pros and cons of several common formats.

JPEG

JPEG is short for "Joint Photographic Experts Group"—but don't worry, everyone uses just the acronym (so you won't have to remember that tongue-twister)! You'll also see this format referred to as JPG, and JPEG images usually end with the .jpg extension under Windows.

- **Pros:** The JPEG format produces high-resolution images that are very small; for example, you can easily fit a typical one-megapixel image in about 200K of hard drive space. JPEG images can also be compressed at varying levels, a trick most digital cameras use when you adjust the photo quality.

- **Cons:** At higher compression levels, a JPEG image can lose a significant amount of detail. (More on this limitation later in this chapter.)

- **Applications:** Because of the space savings, most digital cameras save images in JPEG format. JPEG is also a preferred image format for pictures on the Web (as well as e-mail attachments), because it takes less time to transfer them over a standard dial-up modem.

GIF

GIF, short for "Graphics Interchange Format," was the first popular image format—it dates back to the bulletin board systems and online services of the '80s and early '90s. (If you're old enough to remember CompuServe, then you probably also remember the days when GIF was king.) Images in this format usually end with the .gif extension under Windows.

- **Pros:** GIF images are compressed, but they won't lose data like a JPEG image when repeatedly edited and saved. GIF images are also the only format that can be easily animated for use in Web browsers.

- **Cons:** GIF images are larger than JPEG photographs, and they have a maximum of 256 colors (or 8-bit color) in an image—for printing and onscreen display, the 24-bit color depth (16 million colors) offered by the JPEG format is far better.

- **Applications:** The animation properties of a GIF image make it a natural choice for creating Web pages, but that's about it—the GIF format is rapidly becoming outmoded because of its limited color depth.

BMP

Most Windows users will recognize the Windows bitmap image format—Microsoft uses this format for the pictures that you display on your desktop. These images end with the extension .bmp.

- **Pros:** Bitmap images are usually not compressed, so they deliver superb quality, with both 24-bit color and true grayscale. Their universal compatibility with Microsoft operating systems makes them a good choice for trading images with others using Windows, and virtually every image editor on the planet recognizes the format.

- **Cons:** Bitmap images are also huge — a typical megapixel bitmap image can easily hit three or four megabytes in size.

- **Applications:** Most digital photographers have used bitmap format for archival storage at one time or another. However, the sheer size of bitmap photographs makes them less popular on the Internet and Web than JPEG images.

TIFF

TIFF, short for "Tagged Image File Format," is a popular cross-platform image format that's well-supported by Windows, MacOS, and Linux. These images end with the extension .tif in the Windows world.

- **Pros:** TIFF images can be both compressed or uncompressed, and they offer both 24-bit color and true grayscale. They also provide CMYK color channels — in plain English, this means TIFF images are suitable for color separations, which are used by professional printers and service bureaus.

- **Cons:** TIFF images are significantly larger than JPEG images.

- **Applications:** TIFF is a good all-around image format used by publishers, printing shops and graphic artists — it's not suitable for Web pages, and it's too large for creating e-mail attachments, but TIFF images are recognized by a wide range of image editors and operating systems.

Converting Images

Now that you've been introduced to the image formats you're likely to meet, let's consider a very common scenario you might encounter with a friend

or family member: For example, suppose that you'd like to send your aunt an image from your camera. You attach it in e-mail — a procedure already introduced in the QuickStart at the beginning of the book, plus I'll also show you later in the book. Your aunt receives the photograph just fine, but when she clicks it, Windows 95 tells her that the image file is unrecognized. What can you do?

The problem is simple — your aunt doesn't have an image editor installed on her computer, and the image you sent was in JPEG format, a format that's not directly supported by Windows 95. Therefore, her computer can't open the file to display it.

Let's use Paint Shop Pro to fix the problem. Follow these steps to convert a file from one format to another (in this case, we'll use Windows bitmap, which every version of Windows can display):

1. Click File and select the Open menu item to load your image into Paint Shop Pro.

2. Once you've opened the photograph, click File and choose Save As to display the dialog box shown in Figure 10.1.

3. Click the Save as Type drop-down list box and choose the format for the new image — for our example, choose Windows or OS/2 bitmap (*.bmp).

4. If you like, type a new file name into the File Name field. (Because you're changing the file type, which changes the extension, you won't overwrite the original image.)

Figure 10.1 The Paint Shop Pro Save As dialog box.

Figure 10.2 Setting save options for our converted file.

5. Click the Options button to select the settings the program will use when converting to the new format, and click OK to accept them. Figure 10.2 illustrates the Save Options for the Windows bitmap format. (Most of these settings are different for each format — however, the defaults should work fine, so you shouldn't need to change these unless there's a specific reason.)

6. Click Save to start the conversion and save the new file to disk.

Now you can send the Windows bitmap image to your aunt, and she can display it by simply double-clicking the file icon.

▲ Tip

The later the version of Microsoft Windows, the more image file formats it's likely to recognize. For example, Windows 98 and Windows Me both include an image display program that can open JPEG and TIFF files. If you'd rather not upgrade your copy of Windows, just install an image-display or image-editing program that supports these formats.

The Importance of Compression

I mentioned compression earlier in Chapter 2, where I told you that most digital cameras offer different levels of compression (typically called "photo quality"). I've also told you that applying heavy compression to an image significantly reduces its quality. Let's take a moment to illustrate this effect.

Figure 10.3 "Relic" — a sign of changing times.

As a reference, Figure 10.3 represents an uncompressed bitmap image; that's the sign from the last drive-in movie theater in my hometown, which has since been leveled for a parking lot. (Sigh.) Anyway, notice the sharp edges of the lettering and the shadows. This image takes up about 3.7MB on my hard drive. As you can imagine, that's simply an unacceptable file size for a typical 8MB memory card!

Now let's convert this image to JPEG (a much more efficient image format) and apply 20 percent compression — the result is Figure 10.4. Not really an appreciable amount of difference to your eye, is there? Fact is, I typically use about a 15 percent compression level on my JPEGs, and I've never been able to tell it's there. Now comes the important part: *the file has suddenly dropped in size to a mere 211K!* This level of compression is approximately equal to the "Fine" photo quality on most digital cameras.

Figure 10.4 We've now converted the image to JPEG and compressed it 20 percent.

Figure 10.5 The same image at 70 percent compression.

Next, let's convert "Relic" to a JPEG and apply a whopping 70 percent compression — this is typically the level that most digital cameras use for "Standard" photo quality. By studying Figure 10.5, you can begin to see degradation in detail and sharpness. On the other hand, we've reached 75K in size.

Finally, I thought I would show you what "Relic" looks like at the maximum compression rate of 99 percent, as shown in Figure 10.6. As you can see, even at this incredibly heavy compression rate, the JPEG image format can still deliver the highlights of the image. You can also tell why many graphic artists like to experiment with compression as a creative tool. The size of the image has shrunk to a svelte 23K, too — quite a difference from the 3.7MB we started out with in Figure 10.3.

So what have we learned here? JPEG is the most popular image format available today for a good reason, but watch out — If you continue to compress a JPEG image by 15 percent each time you edit it, you will eventually lose the detail that every digital photographer craves.

To avoid this problem with a file that you open and edit repeatedly, you should adjust your image editor to prevent additional compression each time you save the photograph. For instance, when saving a JPEG image by using Paint Shop Pro, use the Save As command under the File menu instead of simply saving it, and then click the Options button on the Save As dialog box to display the settings shown in Figure 10.7. If the photograph was already in compressed JPEG format, you can reduce the compression to zero before saving it again with the same file name.

Figure 10.6 Is it art? With 99 percent JPEG compression, it just might be!

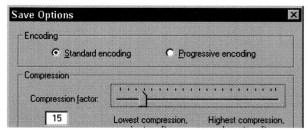

Figure 10.7 Reducing compression keeps your photos healthy!

Preparing Pictures

Most digital photographers have a certain set of needs for their images — for example, you might be interested in traditional uses, such as displaying your work or incorporating it into a presentation or company document. On the other hand, you may be creating a Web site, or you may want to send your digital photographs to others through e-mail.

Each of these applications has a slightly different set of requirements, so in this section I outline the steps you have to take to prepare your images.

Preparing photos for the Web

Although fast DSL and cable modem Internet connections are becoming more commonplace every day, most visitors to your Web site will still be using a traditional analog modem over a telephone line. The "speed bottleneck" created by huge image files helps determine these steps you should take with the photos you'll be adding to your Web pages:

- **Reduce color depth to 256.** To reduce the total file size of your image (and to be compatible with the widest range of computers and browser software), reduce your Web images to 256 colors.

- **Convert to JPEG or GIF format.** These file formats can be compressed to save downloading time.

- **Compress those images.** As I discussed earlier in the chapter, compress your images by 20 to 30 percent.

- **Reduce size as much as possible.** Crop your images as small as you can without losing their visual impact, or resize them smaller to save bytes. Your online visitors will thank you!

Preparing photos for e-mail

Again, the size limitations placed on e-mail attachments by most Internet service providers are a big factor here, but, unlike images for your Web pages, you'd rather that the folks on the receiving end of the e-mail get the best possible photo quality. Therefore, follow these guidelines:

- **Convert to JPEG format.** With a JPEG image, you can usually keep your image below 500K, which is the maximum e-mail attachment size for many ISPs.

- **Reduce the size as much as possible.** Reduce the size of your attachment even further by cropping unnecessary background from your photograph.

Preparing photos for documents

No Internet size constraints here! Instead, you're storing your images on your hard drive and importing them into your presentations and word-processing files. Take these steps to prepare your images:

- **Convert to TIFF or bitmap format.** TIFF and bitmap images are supported as imported pictures by the widest range of office applications, and they deliver the best image quality.

- **Resize or crop your images.** With these images, you also have the luxury of resizing to expand an image as well as cropping. (Most word-processing, presentation, and printing applications can also resize an image after it's been imported into your document, so you probably won't even need your image editor.)

Preparing photos for display

Finally, take these steps for images that you plan to print and display (or images that you're ready to archive on a CD-R disc):

- **Convert to grayscale.** I'll be showing you how to do this in the next chapter — you can easily turn that mundane color photograph into a real eye-catching black-and-white work of art! For example, look at Figure 10.8 — suddenly, I've turned "Relic" into a black-and-white shot.

- **Resize or crop your images.** You can resize your images to expand them so that they'll fit the frame you have in mind — but remember, resizing them too much will incur a penalty in detail and resolution. Also, don't forget to crop unwanted material from your images before you store them or print them.

Figure 10.8 Who needs an expensive 35mm film camera to create stunning black-and-white photography?

Summary

In this chapter, I opened up the Pandora's Box of image formats — you learned which are best for different applications, the advantages and disadvantages of each, and how to convert an image from one format to another. I also demonstrated the importance of compression — including the positive effects of just the right amount and the negative effects of too much compression.

Coming up next, I devote Chapter 11 to one of my favorite computer applications — image editing with Paint Shop Pro.

I f you've been using a traditional film camera until now, it's time you learned about the digital photographer's secret weapon—it can turn a mediocre image into a work of art, or correct mistakes that you didn't see when composing the scene. Of course, I'm talking about the *image editor,* a software application that enables you to make all sorts of adjustments to your digital photographs (both major and minor).

This chapter demonstrates all of the basic procedures you need to deliver better digital images.

Our Tool of Choice: Paint Shop Pro

Your digital camera probably came bundled with an image-editing program—in this chapter, I'll use one of the most popular image editors on the market today, Paint Shop Pro from Jasc Software (www.jasc.com). Figure 11.1 shows you the main menu from Version 7, the latest update to this editor.

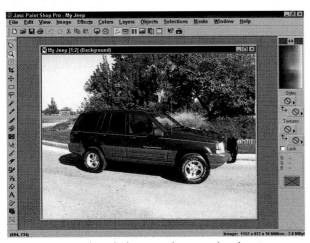

Figure 11.1 A digital photograph opened within Paint Shop Pro.

Paint Shop Pro began as a simple shareware package back in the early '90s, and it has since matured into a very powerful editor with many of the features of Adobe Photoshop. You can download the evaluation version of the program from the company's Web site, which is fully functional for 30 days so you can try out all the tricks I'll show you in this chapter. You can also buy and download the full commercial version of the program from the company's Web site for $99.

One other feature stands out within Paint Shop Pro—the online help for this program is excellent! Each function and procedure is fully explained, making it a good choice for image editing novices.

Solving Minor Problems

Ready to go? Then let's start with three commonplace problems that a digital photographer is often likely to encounter.

Cropping

Cropping a photograph removes a portion of the border of the image—it's a perfect way to remove that door frame from a family photo, or the tail from the family dog that somehow ended up next to the prom portrait! Follow these steps to crop an image in Paint Shop Pro:

1. Click File and select the Open menu item. Locate and click the image file name, and then click Open to load your image into Paint Shop Pro.

2. Once you've opened the photograph you want, click the geometric selection tool at the left of the screen—it looks like a dotted rectangle. Notice that your mouse cursor changes from an arrow to a crosshair icon for more precise alignment.

3. Click the top-left corner of the area you wish to save, and hold the mouse down to drag the selection rectangle to the lower-right corner of the area you want to save. Release the mouse button to select the area, as shown in Figure 11.2.

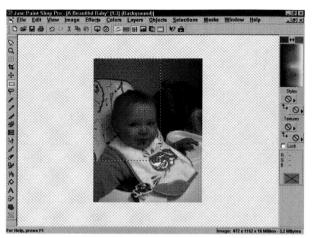

Figure 11.2 Let's get rid of that chair at the side of the frame by cropping it out.

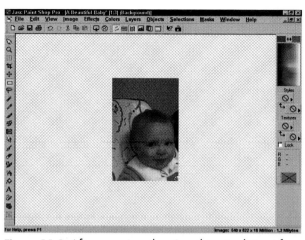

Figure 11.3 After cropping, there's nothing to distract from the baby.

4. Click Image and select the Crop to Selection menu item (or press the Shift+R keyboard shortcut). The area outside the selection rectangle is removed, as shown in Figure 11.3.

5. Don't forget to save your image! Click File and then choose Save (to overwrite the old photograph) or Save As (to save a new image with another file name and/or format).

Reducing red-eye

To remove that aggravating red shine from a subject's eyes, follow these steps:

1. Click File and select the Open menu item to load your image into Paint Shop Pro.

2. Once you've opened the photograph, click Effects, and then choose Enhance Photo and Red-eye Removal from the pop-up menus. Paint Shop Pro displays the Red-eye Removal dialog box shown in Figure 11.4.

3. If your subject's eyes are not in the selection windows, click within the right window and drag the image in the desired direction.\

4. Once the eyes are in the window, click the mouse cursor on the eye in the left window to

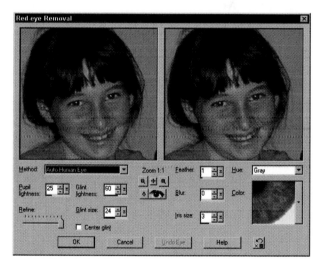

Figure 11.4 We're ready to select the girl's eyes to remove the effects of red-eye.

select it — Paint Shop Pro surrounds the colored portion of the eye with a selection box.

5. Click the Hue drop-down list box and the arrow next to the Color box to choose a replacement eye hue and color.

6. Click OK to replace the red-eye.

7. Repeat Steps 2 through 6 to fix the other eye. The results are great, as you can see in the corrected image in Figure 11.5.

Figure 11.5 Say goodbye to red-eye!

8. Save your changes. Click File and then choose Save (to overwrite the old photograph) or Save As (to save a new image with another file name and/or format).

Adjusting gamma correction

If an image is too light or dark overall, then it's probably a good idea to experiment with gamma correction, which is a group of settings that controls all of the tones within an image. Follow these steps:

1. Click File and select the Open menu item to load your image into Paint Shop Pro.

2. Once you've opened the photograph, click Colors, and then choose Adjust and Gamma Correction from the pop-up menus. Paint Shop Pro displays the Gamma Correction dialog box shown in Figure 11.6.

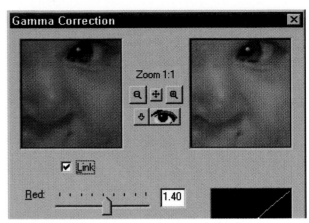

Figure 11.6 The Gamma Correction dialog box.

3. Make sure that the Link checkbox is enabled, and click and drag any of the three slider controls to the right (to lighten the image) or to the left (to darken the image). The window on the right provides a preview of the effects of the correction.

4. When the correction appears correct, click OK.

5. Save your changes. Click File and then choose Save (to overwrite the old photograph) or Save As (to save a new image with another file name and/or format).

> **△ Tip**
> Dissatisfied with the results of a procedure? You can always back up to the previous state of the image by selecting Undo from the Edit menu.

Changing Image Size

If an image needs resizing, follow these steps with Paint Shop Pro:

1. Click File and select the Open menu item to load your image into Paint Shop Pro.

2. Click Image and choose Resize. Paint Shop Pro displays the Resize dialog box shown in Figure 11.7.

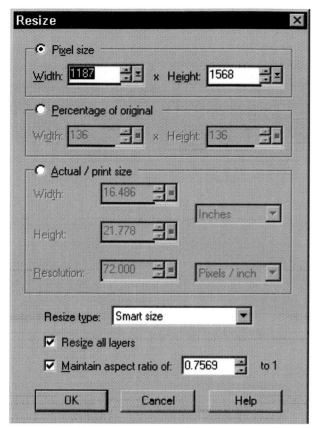

Figure 11.7 Choosing a new size for an image.

3. Paint Shop Pro offers you three options to resize your images: by pixel resolution (the image dimension in pixels), as a percentage of the original size, and the actual size of the final image. I almost always use pixel resolution—enter the new width and height for the image in pixels.

▲ **Tip**

You'll notice that if you enter one number in either width or height, the other value is automatically calculated — this is because the Maintain aspect ratio checkbox at the bottom of the dialog box is enabled, and Paint Shop Pro has already calculated the correct ratio. (The *aspect ratio* is the ratio of the image's height to its width.) To preserve the appearance of the image after you've resized it, I strongly recommend that you leave this box checked unless you need to force an image to a new aspect ratio; a picture can be badly stretched or pinched if the aspect ratio is incorrect.

4. Click the Resize Type drop-down list box and choose Smart size.

5. Click OK to begin resizing the image — the progress bar at the bottom of the window tells you how far you are in the operation. (The larger the image, or the larger the resized image, the more time resizing takes.)

6. Once the image has been resized, save your changes. Click File, and then choose Save (to overwrite the old photograph) or Save As (to save a new image with another file name and/or format).

Changing Image Orientation

If you snap a photograph holding your camera on its end, you may need to change the orientation of the image before it will display correctly. To do so, follow these steps with Paint Shop Pro:

1. Click File and select the Open menu item to load your image into Paint Shop Pro.

2. Click Image and choose Rotate to display the Rotate dialog box shown in Figure 11.8.

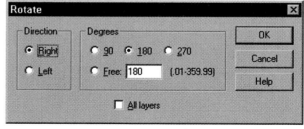

Figure 11.8 Rotating an image to change its orientation is easy with Paint Shop Pro.

3. Choose the direction of rotation by clicking Left or Right. (For my cameras, I always rotate right.)

4. Click the number of degrees to rotate — typically, this is either 90 or 180 degrees.

5. Click OK to rotate the image.

6. Save your changes. Click File and then choose Save (to overwrite the old photograph) or Save As (to save a new image with another file name and/or format).

Changing Color Depth

I discussed reducing the color depth of an image in the previous chapter—here's how you do it:

1. Click File and select the Open menu item to load your image.

2. Click Colors and choose Decrease Color Depth.

3. Choose the desired new color depth from the pop-up menu to display the dialog box shown in Figure 11.9.

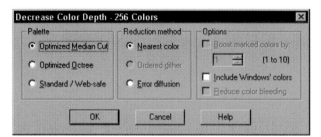

Figure 11.9 The Decrease Color Depth dialog box for a reduction to 256 colors.

4. For Web images, choose Standard / Web-safe—otherwise, choose Optimized Median Cut.

5. For Web images, choose Nearest Color—otherwise, choose Error Diffusion.

6. Click OK.

7. After the process has finished, save your changes. Click File and then choose Save (to overwrite the old photograph) or Save As (to save a new image with another file name and/or format).

Solving Big Problems

Paint Shop Pro can also make dramatic improvements in photographs that would otherwise be ready for the Recycle Bin.

Converting color to grayscale

If the colors are completely wrong for your subject—for example, if Aunt Flo has mismatched her purple and green again—or if you think your image would look better as a black-and-white photograph, you can use Paint Shop Pro to convert it. Follow these steps:

1. Click File and select the Open menu item to load your image.

2. Click Colors and choose Grey Scale.

3. Click File and then choose Save (to overwrite the old photograph) or Save As (to save a new image with another file name and/or format).

Copying and pasting pixels

Do you need to copy a section of your image and paste it elsewhere in the photo, or even paste that portion into another photo, as I did in Chapter 1? Follow these steps:

1. Click File and select the Open menu item to load your image.

2. Click the geometric selection tool at the left of the screen.

3. Click the top-left corner of the area you wish to save, and hold the mouse down to drag the selection rectangle to the lower-right corner of the area you want to save. Release the mouse button to select the area.

4. Click Edit and select the Copy menu item. Windows has now placed the portion of the image that you selected on the clipboard.

5. To paste the contents of the clipboard into the current image, click Edit and choose Paste as New Selection. Paint Shop Pro

enables you to place the selected area any-where in the photograph—just click as soon as you've positioned it where you want it.

6. To paste the contents of the clipboard into another image, click File and choose Close. (Unless you've altered the source image and you want to save those modifications, click No when prompted to save changes.) Click File and Open to open the target image, and then click Edit and choose Paste as New Selection. Click as soon as you've positioned the selected area where you want it.

7. Click File and then choose Save (to overwrite the old photograph) or Save As (to save a new image with another file name and/or format).

Coloring pixels

Although I showed you how to correct red-eye ear-lier, you may need to change the color of individual pixels in an image from time to time—this can erase a portion of the image, or correct a flaw that you can't crop out. Follow these steps to change the color of certain pixels:

1. Click File and select the Open menu item to load your image.

2. Click the zoom tool at the left of the screen—it looks like a magnifying glass.

3. Click the area of the image you need to change to zoom in—continue clicking to zoom closer until you can easily see the area of pixels that needs to be altered. You can also zoom out by right-clicking.

4. Now move your mouse cursor to the top-right corner of the screen and move it over the color you want to use—you'll notice that the cursor changes to an eyedropper. Click once to set the foreground color and right-click once to set the background color—now you're ready to edit.

Tip

To use the actual color in the surrounding pixels, click the eyedropper tool at the left of the screen. Move your eyedropper cursor over the pixel with the color you want to use. Click once with the left mouse button, and once with the right button to "lock in" the colors.

5. Click the paintbrush tool at the left of the screen and move it over the pixel(s) that you need to change. Click to "paint" the pixel and repeat as necessary.

Tip

Remember, if you make a mistake you can undo the effects of your last click by selecting Undo from the Edit Menu.

6. Click File and then choose Save (to overwrite the old photograph) or Save As (to save a new image with another file name and/or format).

Sharpening fuzzy subjects

Although it's definitely easier to focus a shot cor-rectly than fix it afterwards, sometimes you'll find yourself with a great picture that's somewhat blurry. Unless you're looking for a soft focus effect, you can use Paint Shop Pro to rescue the image and sharpen it—think of the process as increasing the contrast at the edges of the subject. However, it's important to note that this *does not* add detail, so sharpening can only work so much magic; it's wise to try this trick only once or twice on an image, or it will end up looking worse! Follow these steps:

1. Click File and select the Open menu item to load your image into Paint Shop Pro.

2. Once you've opened the photograph, click Effects and then choose Sharpen and Sharpen More from the pop-up menus.

3. Save your changes. Click File and then choose Save (to overwrite the old photograph) or Save As (to save a new image with another file name and/or format).

Summary

This chapter offered a quick primer on image editing with Paint Shop Pro—I demonstrated everything you need to do to make major and minor changes to your photographs. Although the program has dozens of other features, you're likely to use the procedures I covered over and over; I'll show you many of the artistic effects you can create in Chapter 15.

Next, we'll cover suggestions and tips for candid photographs.

PART **IV**

→ Digital Photography Projects

Candid Photography Projects

IN THIS CHAPTER • Candid photography tour

• Tips and tricks for candid photography

So exactly what is candid photography? Actually, the answer is simple: just about any type of photograph that you take with little or no time to pose the subject(s) beforehand! It's the art of capturing a moment or taking someone's portrait "on the fly." Many photographers will tell you that candid shots are the hardest of all to take — you have to be ready to compose a good photograph within just a few seconds, as well as juggle manual settings if you're setting exposure or focus.

This chapter offers a number of tips you can follow for better candid shots — and I show you some great candid photography.

A Tour of Candid Photography

We've all taken candid photographs of friends and family — they usually make up the bulk of your family album, but they're usually not composed according to the rules we covered earlier in the book. Remember, the spontaneity of a candid shot doesn't necessarily prevent you from taking a few seconds to compose your scene! If you can apply the tips I provide in this chapter, you won't even have to interrupt the action around you — and the chances that you might snap a great photograph are greatly increased.

Children

Babies and young children are the classic subjects of candid photography. After all, it's very hard to get them to pose anyway! If you can catch a young child making a mess, as shown in Figure 12.1, you're practically assured of success.

Here's another tip for babies and toddlers: they make great subjects when they're asleep, as in Figure 12.2.

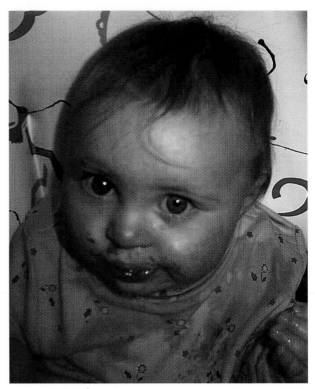

Figure 12.1 What a mess. . . .

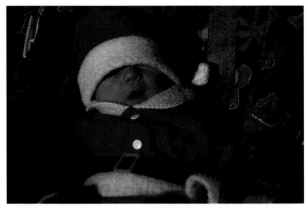

Figure 12.2 "Sleepy Santa." Photograph by Michael D. Welch.

Photographing the everyday actions of a child has its rewards — would a grown-up subject let you take the great shot in Figure 12.3? I don't think so!

Figure 12.3 That cake never had a chance.

Animals

Candid portraits with animals are another favorite, as in Figure 12.4 — notice also how the photographer balanced and contrasted the two subjects.

Figure 12.4 "A new Westie puppy." Photograph by Michael D. Welch.

Every pet owner has a favorite moment captured on film — if your pet is asleep or at rest, move slowly and quietly. Because pets are drawn to you, it can be difficult to catch them in action; however, it's easy to grab a candid image, such as the one in Figure 12.5, where your pet is approaching you. You can also photograph your pet playing with others or sleeping.

Figure 12.5 "Dinnertime!"

With a telephoto lens, wildlife shots, such as the squirrel shown in Figure 12.6, can become a lifetime hobby. The speed of a wild animal, the requirements of existing light, and the need to focus accurately within a couple of seconds can add up to a real challenge for photographers of all experience levels. Consider a digital camera with manual focus and exposure control, a fast shutter speed, and burst mode so you can set your camera for a particular scene without the delay caused by automatic mechanisms. Unless you have the patience of a hunter, I recommend a trip to the zoo, where you're very likely to snap a good photograph.

Figure 12.6 *"Western gray squirrel, Golden Gate Park, San Francisco."* Photograph by Michael D. Welch.

Culture

As I mentioned earlier, you may often have the luxury of posing the subject in a candid photograph by having the person sit down for a second or two—especially if you've familiarized yourself with your camera and can snap the shot quickly, as I recommended early in the book.

Although Figure 12.7 is an excellent example of the woman's unique dress and jewelry, it also captures her nobility and wisdom—the background is very basic, and the scene couldn't be simpler, so it really illustrates what you can do with a candid shot of a seated subject. Visual differences in culture

always make an interesting photograph, yet some candid shots show more than that; this photograph reveals an entirely different slice of life.

Figure 12.7 *"Native American, Monument Valley, Utah."* Photograph by Michael D. Welch.

With candid photos, keep in mind that there's no time for metering, pacing off a distance estimate, or lengthy preparation, so you'll be at the mercy of existing lighting conditions and your camera's built-in flash. Or in the case of my Bourbon Street night scene in Figure 12.8, it may turn out better if you disable your camera's flash. The vibrant colors highlighting timeless architecture—a candid picture such as this can transport you hundreds or thousands of miles in an instant!

Figure 12.8 "New Orleans at Night."

Figure 12.9 A candid portrait with a great background.

Backgrounds

Keep your "photographer's eye" open for vivid and interesting backgrounds — they can make a simple candid portrait into something special, as in Figure 12.9. The subject simply turned to face the camera. The lighting and spectacular flowers did the rest!

If you've taken your camera on trips, then you may have been lucky enough to encounter a mountain vista. Too often, a novice photographer makes the mistake of framing more of such a background than the subject — that's the moment to consider a scenic photograph instead.

Summary

The photographs in this gallery show you what's possible with a digital camera and a few seconds of composition — by following the tips I outlined, you can turn a typical candid snapshot into a truly memorable image, even if you're using a fully-automatic "point-and-shoot" camera with a fixed-focus lens!

Next, I'll turn our attention to scenic photography.

CHAPTER 13

Scenic Photography Projects

IN THIS CHAPTER • Scenic photography tour

• Tips and tricks for scenic photography

In the previous chapter, I discussed tips for candid photographs — but in this chapter, your subjects won't be moving. Scenic photography captures the beauty of the landscape around you, both natural and man-made. Although other minor elements may appear within the frame, the subject is actually the background itself.

Get ready for some outstanding examples of scenic photography — and I'll include tips and tricks you can use to help you produce better scenic images on your next trip or vacation.

A Tour of Scenic Photography

If you're wondering whether you need an expensive camera stuffed full of manual controls to take a good scenic photograph, rest easy: Even the simplest "point-and-shoot" automatic digital camera with a fixed-focus lens can take spectacular scenic shots, because that lens can focus to the horizon.

Natural beauty

The digital photograph I took in Figure 13.1 captures a small waterfall and the natural cavern next to it — but don't think that it didn't require composition to pull the tree in the foreground and the waterfall into the Rule of Thirds! This is actually the third angle I tried, and it proved to be the only one that afforded a clear view through the brush and trees.

Here's the moral of the story: Unless you want to capture specific lighting at a certain time of day, you have plenty of time to compose and experiment while taking a scenic photograph. Of course, a mountain range won't look that different if you walk another hundred feet along the trail — but you might find the perfect trees to frame it.

Figure 13.2 is another illustration of scenic composition: Michael could have simply shot Mt. Rainier by itself, but he positioned himself to take advantage of the stand of tall pines. Notice also the trail pulling you into the image and the hikers to give

human interest, the sharp contrast of green against the brilliant white, and the sharp verticals of the pines against the horizontal vista of the mountain. A good photograph becomes a great photograph!

Figure 13.1 "Arkansas Waterfall."

Figure 13.2 "Hikers at Mt. Rainier, Washington." Photograph by Michael D. Welch.

Nature provides countless textures for scenic images. As you develop your "photographer's eye," you'll see them everywhere from exotic climes (as in Figure 13.3) to your own backyard (as in Figure 13.4).

Figure 13.4 "Tree Bones — near Mammoth, California." Photograph by Michael D. Welch.

Figure 13.3 "Death Valley Dune, California." Photograph by Michael D. Welch.

Man-made scenes

Spectacular man-made scenery is another staple of a digital photographer's collection — that covers shots of monuments, ruins, massive structures, and artwork on a grand scale. The photograph in Figure 13.5 is a favorite of mine, capturing the beauty of sky, water, rock, and the buildings around Hoover Dam in a single scene. This image captures a different view of the dam from an unusual angle (the traditional shot you generally see is toward the dam itself), and it helps accentuate the contrast between the awesome natural beauty of the river and the technological achievements that surround it.

Figure 13.5 "View from Hoover Dam."

Even a simple road winding through the country-side makes a statement—notice how the figures in the foreground corner help to deliver a sense of scale to the scene in Figure 13.6, while the curve of the road works to draw the viewer into the image.

Figure 13.6 "Walking in a Peninsula Open Space Preserve, Northern California." Photograph by Michael D. Welch.

The pueblo buildings in Figure 13.7 have all the elements of a great image: color, texture, geometry, and shadow. The person at the top adds an extra element to improve the photo.

Figure 13.7 "Taos Pueblo, Colorado." Photograph by Michael D. Welch.

Clouds and sky

Another source of both pattern and color is always available—directly above your head! Who hasn't marveled at one time or another at the sky above? Whether you shoot a scene at dusk with the surrounding woods in silhouette, as in Figure 13.8, or clouds eclipsing the sun as in Figure 13.9, cloud patterns and the sky can result in very dramatic photographs. For the night image, I disabled my camera's flash to enhance the silhouette effect; to shoot cloud patterns, try bracketing with manual exposure settings.

Figure 13.8 "Missouri Woods at Dusk."

Figure 13.9 "Sunstreaks from a Backlit Cloud, Northern California." Photograph by Michael D. Welch.

The mist and sunlight in Figure 13.10 create the mood—and with the ferry providing a reference for the scale of the scene, the image is worthy of any gallery.

Figure 13.11 "Bean Hollow State Beach, California." Photograph by Michael D. Welch.

Some preparations for a good photograph take longer—but I think you'll agree that it was worth the extra time to create the snowman in Figure 13.12!

Figure 13.10 "Crossing Howe Sound, British Columbia." Photograph by Michael D. Welch.

Changing the scenery

If you're considering a scenic shot, it's also fun to improve on the existing scene by adding a dramatic touch. Naturally, this isn't possible all the time, but consider Figure 13.11. By including a simple line of footprints in the soft sand, the photographer has added an entirely new meaning to this scene at the seashore.

Figure 13.12 "Yosemite Falls, California." Photograph by Michael D. Welch.

Summary

Any serious photographer knows that the world around us can provide limitless subjects for a digital camera—and in this chapter, we explored the possibilities of scenic photography. With images like these, you can see why it's always a good idea to carry your camera with you. It's impossible to tell when inspiration may strike!

We've already seen how Paint Shop Pro can solve problems with your photographs, but in Chapter 14 I'll take you on a whirlwind tour of the program's creative power.

 # Image Editing Projects

IN THIS CHAPTER • What are effects and filters?

• How do I install a plug-in?

• A gallery of special effects

In Chapter 11, I showed you how to alter and edit your digital images to solve problems with orientation, size, and composition. Now it's time to harness the power of Paint Shop Pro in another way. By adding effects to your images, you can transform an ordinary photograph into an original work of art.

In this chapter, you'll exercise your creative instincts with digital effects and filters—tools that no film photographer can use!

What are Digital Effects and Filters?

Effects and filters perform the same task—they modify an image in some way, using a mathematical formula. (On the purely technical side, a filter can apply changes to the pixels in an image automatically, whereas an effect usually requires your manual intervention.) Most image editors have at least one or two effects built in, but a program may also enable you to add hundreds of new effects by installing third-party modules—they're usually called *plug-ins*. An effect or filter can usually be controlled, so you can specify the degree of change (and sometimes, even where it will occur within the image).

Paint Shop Pro includes both an Effect Browser and a Filter Browser; these windows make it easy to review the changes that each of your effects and filters will make to an image. Figure 14.1 shows the

Effect Browser—as you click different effects in the list, the preview window to the right displays a thumbnail sample of the new image. To open the browser, click Effects and choose Effect Browser.

How Do I Install a Plug-in?

If your image editor supports plug-ins, you can expand the range of your digital toolbox—first, however, those plug-ins must be installed so that your editor can recognize and use them.

In Paint Shop Pro, follow these steps to add a new plug-in:

1. Click File and select Preferences, and then click File Locations from the pop-up menu. Paint Shop Pro displays the File Locations dialog box.

2. Click the Plug-in Filters tab to display the settings shown in Figure 14.2.

3. Click the Enable Filters checkbox to enable Paint Shop Pro to use external plug-ins.

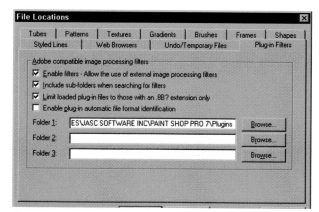

Figure 14.2 Configuring third-party plug-ins within Paint Shop Pro.

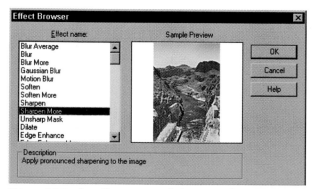

Figure 14.1 The Effect Browser helps you select the right effect to transform an image.

4. Click the Browse button next to the Folder 2 field and select the folder where you've installed the plug-in files. (By default, Folder 1 points to the folder "C:\PROGRAM FILES\JASC SOFTWARE INC\PAINT SHOP PRO 7\Plugins"—you can also install the plug-ins directly to that folder, if you like.)

5.   Click OK to save your changes and return to Paint Shop Pro. The plug-in now appears in your Filter Browser.

Mark's Top Ten Gallery of Effects

Every image editor has different built-in effects. In this section, I show you the results produced by ten of my favorite effects within Paint Shop Pro. The image in Figure 14.3 serves as the starting point for each effect.

To use an effect, either open the Effect Browser or click Effects and choose an effect from the pop-up menu.

Gaussian Blur

At a low radius (the width of the edge that's blurred), Gaussian Blur is great for adding a soft focus to an image—at a higher radius, it produces a blur effect, such as the one shown in Figure 14.4. I used a radius of 3 for this image. Note that applying Gaussian Blur significantly reduces the contrast in your image — therefore, if you're applying more than one effect to a digital photograph it's generally a good idea to apply this filter last.

Figure 14.3 "Steeple" — with no effects added.

Figure 14.4 The effects of Gaussian Blur.

Sharpen

Sharpen can bring out details in your image or help correct minor focusing problems, but be careful — it can also enhance imperfections and add a grainy look to an image if it's overused. Figure 14.5 illustrates the effect of Sharpen More — it's less noticeable on this image, because the original was already well focused. Paint Shop Pro also offers a Clarify function that can help rescue a blurred image from the Recycle Bin. To use Clarify, click Effects and choose Enhance Photo; then select Clarify from the pop-up menu. Like other filters, you can preview the results of the Clarify operation before you apply it.

Noise

The Noise effect yields an interesting "rainbow grain" to an image, as shown in Figure 14.6. I used a 50 percent uniform noise pattern on this image. I like to use the Noise filter whenever I want to create a dramatic effect, but at the same time, to keep the subject recognizable — for example, when I want to preserve most of the detail and contrast areas in an image.

Figure 14.5 The effects of Sharpening.

Figure 14.6 The effects of Noise.

Buttonize

I have a lot of fun with this one — it's great for making thumbnail-sized "buttons" for your Web pages or adding a quick frame to an image that I'm sending to someone. The example in Figure 14.7 used a transparent edge with a 75 percent opaque level. The effect is less noticeable on the dark edges of this photo, but Buttonize can be very effective on certain images. You can also select the height and width of the edge — selecting a solid edge can produce a simple but effective 3D picture frame.

Figure 14.7 The effects of Buttonize.

Black Pencil

This effect produces an image that packs quite a visual punch, as you can see in Figure 14.8. If you're like me and you can't even draw a stick figure, use Black Pencil for an "instant sketch." Again, this is another dramatic filter that can preserve virtually all of the detail in the image. To create an interesting texture effect, lower the opacity setting (which increases the contrast used on the darker areas in the image).

Figure 14.8 The effects of Black Pencil.

Neon Glow

Make your subject glow from within against a nighttime sky! Figure 14.9 shows the steeple image with Neon Glow set to 80 percent detail and 100 percent opacity. Play around with the settings to see what you get.

Page Curl

Here's another effect that's popular for Web pages — you can vary the area and size of the curl, too. Figure 14.10 shows the result of the Page Curl effect. You can select the corner that you'd like to use for the curl, as well as the color of the "underside" of the image — neat!

Figure 14.9 The effects of Neon Glow.

Figure 14.10 The effects of Page Curl.

Ripple

In Figure 14.11, the Ripple effect has turned the surface of the image into water, and we've dropped a "virtual pebble" into the center! Although I usually like the ripple to appear in the center of the image, the location can be adjusted using the Horizontal and Vertical center sliders. Paint Shop Pro also provides you full control over the size and the distance between each wave in your ripple.

Sunburst

This is an especially fitting addition for our original image, which was taken on an overcast day. With the Sunburst effect shown in Figure 14.12, I've added a real-looking flash of sunlight behind the church, complete with lens reflections! (Actually, most photographers try to avoid lens reflections, also called *flare* — and I prefer the overcast sky because it enabled me to capture the detail of the stonework — but we're exercising our creative side now.) To add color to your sunburst — say, for example, for a photo of a sunset — click in the Color box to display the color palette and then click on the desired shade.

Figure 14.11 The effects of Ripple.

Figure 14.12 The effects of Sunburst.

Mirror

My final favorite effect, Mirror, has doubled the size of the church! I use this effect often for portraits and macro close-ups. Figure 14.13 shows the Mirror effect in action. You're not limited to adding a reflection straight down the center of your image, however; Paint Shop Pro also allows you to specify the horizontal and vertical offset for the mirror, as well as the angle of rotation for the reflection.

Figure 14.13 The effects of Mirror.

Remember, I've covered only ten of my favorite effects here — Paint Shop Pro offers dozens more, so I recommend that you use the Effect Browser and experiment! On the other hand, just because the effects are there doesn't mean that you need to change all your photos with them. They're great when they're right for your image or for the result you're trying to produce, but they can also be over-done. To find out when they're right, have fun experimenting.

Summary

This chapter explored the creative side of Paint Shop Pro by trying out ten different effects. You saw a cross-section of the exotic artwork that anyone can create with just a few mouse clicks.

Chapter 15 leads you step-by-step through a number of popular projects — you'll have some real fun with your digital photographs!

Making Crafts with Your Photographs

IN THIS CHAPTER
- Printing a T-shirt transfer
- Adding a windows background
- Creating a custom wine label

Traditional film photography is usually a pure art form — you snap a photograph, develop it, and then enjoy it framed or as part of an album collection. You might already associate one or two crafts with film prints, such as collage or decoupage, but virtually all photographs produced from a negative remain as they are.

On the other hand, I'm happy to tell you that static display is *not* the end result of a digital photograph! In fact, my experience is just the opposite with a digital image — it very rarely remains on your hard drive or stored on a CD-ROM simply for display on your monitor. Mix in an inkjet printer or another computer program, such as an e-mail application, stir well, and you'll end up with a completely new medium for transmitting and displaying your image.

In the projects presented in this chapter, I assume that you've already taken great photos with your digital camera and that you're ready to have more fun with your images than just admiring them. Let's go to work!

Printing a T-Shirt Transfer

Visit your local mall, and you're likely to see at least one kiosk that produces custom T-shirts with your picture (and then charges you an arm and a leg). Let's use your inkjet printer and a sheet of transfer paper to create your own personalized shirt at home.

To print a T-shirt transfer, you'll need the following materials:

- T-shirt transfer paper
- Prewashed cotton or cotton/polyester T-shirt (items made from canvas work as well)
- A T-shirt printing program, such as Hanes T-ShirtMaker
- Scissors
- Inkjet printer
- Several sheets of regular inkjet paper
- Sturdy table or countertop
- Sheet or pillowcase
- Clothes iron

Preparing the fabric

Follow these general steps to prepare the fabric for the transfer:

1. Wash the item first in cold water! Don't apply a transfer to a brand new T-shirt.

2. Machine-dry the item at normal temperature without fabric softener.

3. If you like, you can iron the item to help keep it wrinkle-free during the transfer. (No starch or steam, though!) Let the fabric cool to room temperature before applying the transfer.

Printing the design

Warning

USE AN INKJET PRINTER TO PRINT YOUR TRANSFER! Never print a T-shirt transfer on a laser printer — most transfer paper is not designed for laser printers, and you may damage your hardware.

Follow these general steps to print a transfer:

1. Use any application that prints in color to prepare your design — however, the design must be reversed to appear correctly after the transfer has been applied. Most programs especially designed for printing transfers will create this "mirror image" automatically; if the program doesn't reverse the image, check to see if your printer has a "mirror image" or "flip horizontal" option that you can enable. (If your printer offers an "Iron-On" or "Transfer Paper" paper type, it may also reverse the image automatically — check your printer's manual to be sure.)

2. Print a test page using regular paper. It's a good idea to leave at least two inches of border all around the design; this will help ensure that it won't "wrap around" a T-shirt, out of sight. Adjust your design as necessary until it's the right size.

3. Load a sheet of transfer paper into the printer according to the manufacturer's directions.

4. Make the necessary changes to your printer settings — for example, select the option to reverse the image (if necessary) and select Transfer/Iron-On paper in the Printer Setup. It's also a good idea to select the best possible print quality.

5. Print the transfer by selecting the Print command from the File menu in your application.

6. Trim around the edges of the printed design, making sure that you keep a consistent distance from the edge. (It's also a good idea to leave a small "flap" of extra border at one corner so you can easily remove the transfer paper.)

Applying the transfer

> ✏️ **Note**
>
> The settings and specific time periods that I mention in this section apply only to HP Iron-On T-shirt Transfers. Different brands of T-shirt transfers may require other iron settings, or they may require more or less heating time, so follow the instructions that come with your transfers.

To apply a transfer to a cloth item:

1. Choose a table or countertop that's wide enough to provide a hard, smooth backing for the entire item, such as a Formica countertop. Cover this surface with a sheet or pillowcase. Take care to smooth all wrinkles from the fabric.

2. Preheat your iron at its highest setting for 15 minutes.

> ⬇️ **Warning**
>
> Do not use a steam setting on your iron! Steam will not help smooth wrinkles when applying a transfer, and it can damage the special coating on the paper.

3. Arrange the T-shirt or fabric item in the middle of the surface you've prepared. The area to be decorated should be facing up.

4. Align the transfer on top of the T-shirt, printed side down, as shown in Figure 15.1.

Figure 15.1 We're ready to begin ironing.

5. Begin ironing, moving slowly from the top of the design toward the bottom, keeping to the edge of the transfer. Use constant pressure — to avoid overheating, keep the iron moving constantly, and overlap the edges of the transfer with the iron to seal them. If you're using a fabric with a heavy weave, such as canvas, press harder to ensure that the design transfers correctly.

> ▲ **Tip**
>
> The iron should never rest in one place for more than a couple of seconds — the transfer works best if you keep your iron moving!

6. Now move to the other three edges of the design, using the same technique. Don't forget to leave the extra border "flap" unsealed, so you can easily lift the transfer paper when you're finished.

7. Once all four edges have been sealed, iron the center of the design by using a circular motion.

8. Once the center of the design has been sealed, remove the iron and turn it off. Using the unsealed flap, pull the transfer paper slowly from the fabric — you must remove the transfer paper before the fabric has cooled.

9. After the transfer paper has been removed, let the T-shirt cool. You've now got a custom-designed T-shirt!

Adding a Windows Background

There's nothing like a custom background image on your desktop to bring a smile to your face — even on a Monday morning in Cubicleville! Remember, an image must be in Windows bitmap format to use as a background, so you may have to convert a photo before you can use it — and the image must also be saved in the Windows folder on your hard drive.

Once you've saved your bitmap image in the Windows directory, follow these steps:

1. Right-click any empty section of your Windows desktop to open the Display Properties dialog box shown in Figure 15.2.

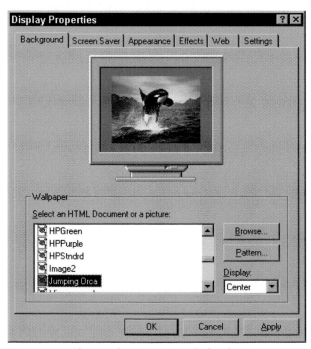

Figure 15.2 The Display Properties dialog box.

2. Click the Background tab.

3. Click the file name for the image you want to use in the Wallpaper list to highlight it.

4. Click OK.

▲ Tip

If you're using a bitmap with a much smaller resolution than your desktop, don't use the Stretch option (in the Display drop-down list) — your image will likely end up very distorted and grainy. Instead, use the Center option (to place it in the middle of the desktop) or the Tile option (to repeat it in a pattern across your desktop).

Creating a Custom Wine Label

Know someone who appreciates a good bottle of wine? Here's a great idea for a special wedding, birthday, or anniversary gift using a digital photograph from your collection: give them a bottle of wine with a label they'll remember!

To create a custom wine label, you'll need the following materials:

- Glossy photo paper
- Paint Shop Pro or other image editor
- Paper cutter or scissors
- Inkjet printer
- Double-sided tape
- Bottle of wine

▲ Tip

Inkjet prints will bleed if they get wet or can be damaged if handled with damp hands. I recommend using laminating film — the kind that doesn't require a special machine or heat. (You can get it at an office supply store.) This way the label is sealed and protected.

Designing and printing your label

To create the label by using Paint Shop Pro, follow these steps:

1. Run Paint Shop Pro and open the image you want to use for the label.

2. Resize the image to about 5 × 4 inches. (Just in case, measure the label on the bottle, and allow for at least half an inch of overlap on all sides.) Click Image and choose Resize, and then click Actual size and enter **5** inches in the Width field, as shown in Figure 15.3. Note that if the Maintain aspect ratio checkbox is enabled, Paint Shop Pro will automatically enter a number in the Height field for you — in this case, my original image resizes very close to four inches in height, so it's fine. Click OK to resize the photo.

▲ **Tip**

Most digital cameras take images with an aspect ratio of about 1.32 to 1, which should enable you to resize with the Maintain aspect ratio checkbox enabled — this prevents your image from being distorted or "stretched." If, however, your image has a different original aspect ratio, you can either crop the image to change the ratio or disable this field and let Paint Shop Pro alter the image to fit (but be prepared for some distortion).

3. Don't forget to add a line of text! Click the Text icon on the toolbar at the left of the Paint Shop Pro icon (the icon looks like a letter A) and then click the cursor where you would like the line of text to begin. Paint Shop Pro displays the Text Entry dialog box shown in Figure 15.4. Choose a font from the Name drop-down list box and a font size from the Size list box, and then click in the Text box and type your message. Click OK to create the text.

4. Make the necessary changes to your printer settings — select Photo paper and the best possible print quality in the Printer Setup.

5. Load a sheet of glossy photo paper in your printer according to the manufacturer's instructions.

6. Click File and select Print to print the label.

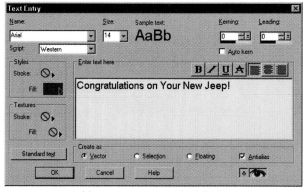

Figure 15.4 Adding text to our wine label.

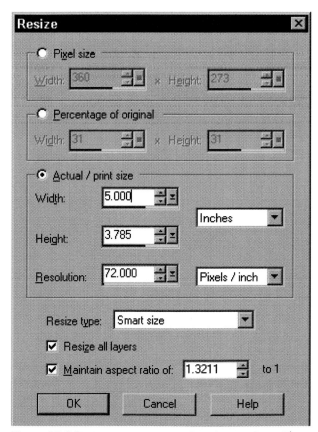

Figure 15.3 Resizing an image to 5 × 4 using Paint Shop Pro.

Applying your label

Follow these steps to apply the label to the bottle:

1. Using a paper cutter or scissors, trim around the edges of the label.

2. Cut a piece of laminating film slightly larger than your label.

3. Peel off the laminating film backing. Carefully center the label and place it face down on the laminating film.

4. Center the laminated label so that it completely covers the existing label on the wine bottle and press down to apply.

5. Smooth the new label with a cloth, moving from the center of the label to the outside edges to remove any air bubbles.

Laminating film seals and protects your custom label from moisture damage.

Summary

This chapter included fun activities you can try with images from your digital camera—they give you an idea of the creative possibilities you can explore with an inkjet printer and how you can display your photographs by using your computer.

Hewlett-Packard Technical Support's Frequently Asked Questions

The material in this appendix has been collected over several years as a "knowledge base" resource by the Hewlett-Packard technical support staff at Customer Care Centers around the world. This appendix includes the most common questions asked by owners of HP digital cameras, as well as the responses to those questions. If you own an HP digital camera, I would highly recommend that you read the appropriate sections of this appendix (even if you're not currently experiencing problems with your unit).

Note

Even if you don't own an HP camera, you'll still find this appendix a valuable resource. Although the following solutions and procedures in this appendix address specific camera models manufactured by Hewlett-Packard, much of this material applies to any camera used on a PC under Windows 95, Windows 98, Windows Me, Windows 2000, or Windows NT, and you can easily adapt the solutions to fit your printer.

My camera is beeping. Is something wrong?

Your camera can beep for a number of reasons, including:

- A beep occurs once when the picture has been successfully taken.

- When the shutter button is pressed if the photo memory card is full or inoperable, the camera beeps as long as the button is pressed.

- When the HP PhotoSmart Digital Camera is already on and a full memory card is inserted, the camera beeps as long as the button is pressed.

- To indicate a full card after the last possible picture is taken, the camera beeps several times.

- When the battery is low, the information LCD empty-battery symbol blinks, and the camera beeps several times.

- At power on, if the memory card is full or inoperable (bad, or unformatted), the camera beeps several times.

Whenever I'm downloading pictures from my camera through a serial connection, my mouse suddenly stops working and I have to reboot. How can I fix this?

By default, the camera software is set to Auto Detect. When this is the case, all serial ports will be checked until the HP PhotoSmart camera responds. In a few cases, a serial pointing device (such as a mouse, a digitizer tablet, or a touchpad) will stop working when its port is checked. To stop this from happening, the camera software needs to be set to check only the port that the camera will use. Here's how to set the software:

1. Connect the HP PhotoSmart Digital Camera to the PC (the camera must be turned off).

2. Open your imaging software and download normally.

3. When the HP PhotoSmart Digital Camera screen opens, the mouse stops functioning. When the message comes up saying that the camera is not responding, use the Tab key to highlight the Comm Port: menu. Use down arrow and up arrow keys to select the COM port where the camera is connected.

Note

If you are not sure which port number your camera is connected to, select COM4 and use the Tab key to select the Connect button, turn the camera on, and then press the Enter key. Repeat this for COM3, and then COM2.

4. Turn the HP PhotoSmart Digital Camera on. Use the Tab key to select the Connect button and press the Enter key.

5. When the HP PhotoSmart Digital Camera is detected, a Save Communication Settings screen comes up asking if this will be the new default setting.

6. Press the Enter key to save the new setting.

7. Press Alt+F4 until the Windows Shut Down window comes up.

8. Use the down arrow key to select Restart the Computer.

9. When Windows comes back up, go back to your imaging software and acquire again.

The camera software will now look for the camera only in the selected port.

Windows 95, 98, NT 4.0, 2000, and Me system errors and what to do about them

System errors are frequently related to memory. The following troubleshooting steps can help you track down and solve memory-related problems. Some of these procedures, particularly the temporary file procedure, are primarily for maintenance and should be performed regularly.

Typical memory related system errors include the following:

- HP PhotoSmart software appears only briefly after a launch and then immediately disappears.

- Software installation halts or aborts.

- Fatal exception or illegal operation errors occur.

- Start–Stop condition occurs (HP PhotoSmart S20 photo scanner).

Shutting down background activities

Many computers load programs during start-up; these programs are launched each time the PC is turned on or restarted. These background activities may slow computer speed, reduce the system resources, or cause lockups, fatal exceptions, illegal operations, or other memory symptoms. As a rule, shut down all background activity during software installation. Here is one approach:

1. Press Ctrl+Alt+Delete to view the Close Program window (for Windows NT, also click Task Manager to view the Task Manager window).

2. The list in the Close Program window represents programs currently running on the computer. Click any program except Explorer (the operating system) to highlight/select it.

3. Click End Task. Some programs have a secondary confirmation message that appears within a few seconds. Click End Task on that message, too.

4. Repeat this sequence until all programs, except Explorer, are terminated.

Note

Each time the computer is restarted, most of the programs you terminated in the preceding steps will return to running in the background. These shut-down steps may need to be repeated if the computer is restarted when software installation is incomplete. A long-term solution may be to clear the Start Up files to prevent the automatic launch of such programs. For more detailed instructions, or, if otherwise necessary, contact the PC manufacturer. In the case of HP computers, contact HP Pavilion or HP Vectra support.

Removing temporary files

Temporary files build up and use hard drive space. These files may be created when closing a program, by improperly shutting down the computer, or they may be deliberately produced by programs. Over time, the amount of hard drive space these files occupy may become significant. They tend to slow or impede your computer's operation. Regular removal of these files frees hard drive space. To clear temporary files, follow these instructions:

1. Click Start.

2. Click Find.

3. Click Files or Folders.

4. In field labeled, Named, enter or type, ***.tmp** (the asterisk acts as a wildcard).

5. In the Look In field, use the drop-down arrow to select the (C:) drive only.

6. Click Find Now. It is okay to delete any files listed here.

7. After deleting the .tmp files, click Start.

8. Click Shut Down.

9. Ensure that Restart the Computer is selected.

10. Click OK.

The .tmp files should no longer affect the memory resources of your computer.

Note

Delete all *.tmp files possible. Occasionally, some .tmp files may not delete.

Creating free space on the C:\ hard drive

The amount of free space available on the C:\ hard drive is critical. As it declines to around 200MB, software installation problems, computer lockups, and fatal exception errors become more likely to occur. The C:/ drive is normally used for the computer's swap file. Adding an additional hard drive will not solve the problem by itself. However, noncritical files on the C:\ drive may be moved to a new hard drive (if applicable) or to offline storage to create some free space. To check for available free space on the C:\ drive, follow these instructions:

1. On the desktop, double-click the My Computer icon.

2. Right-click the (C:) hard drive.

3. Select Properties.

4. If free space is less than 200MB, consider deleting programs that are no longer used, delete .tmp files, and move noncritical programs to a second hard drive.

Loading and running lines on Windows 95, Windows 98, and Windows Me

During computer restart, some programs are launched automatically through the WIN.INI file. It may be necessary to modify the WIN.INI file to temporarily or permanently prevent unwanted programs from running. Here's how:

1. Click Start.

2. Click Run.

3. In the Open entry field, type **win.ini** (using lower case is okay).

4. Click OK.

5. Place a semicolon (;) in front of the `load=` line. This adds a comment to the line, and the computer will not process it at start-up.

6. Create a new blank `load=` line (recommended to prevent Windows from automatically recreating a new `load=` line). Here's how:

   a. Place the cursor at the far right end of the `load=` line that now begins with a semicolon.

   b. Press Enter.

   c. Type **load=** on the new blank line.

   d. Place a semicolon in front of the `run=` line.

7. Create a new blank `run=` line. Here's how:

   a. Place the cursor at the far right end of the `run=` line that now begins with a semicolon.

   b. Press Enter.

   c. Type **run=** on the new blank line.

   d. Click File and then click Save.

My HP PhotoSmart digital camera sometimes records a vertical streak of a solid color across some images. What's happening?

This is a common problem with digital cameras using charge-couple device (CCD) technology. Cells with high-level output (where the image of the sun is located) will affect other cells above and below them by color bleeding. Avoid taking pictures with bright objects in them (for example, the reflection of chrome under direct sunlight, mirrors, or low morning/afternoon sun). Otherwise, the portions blocked by the streaks are unrecoverable.

Whenever I try to download or acquire an image from my camera using an image editor, I get a TWAIN error. Can I fix this?

First, verify that your third-party program can see the scanner or digital camera through its own TWAIN select source. While software applications vary on how to select a TWAIN source, the easiest way to determine whether your program supports TWAIN is to see if an Acquire option appears on the File menu. If not, then check for a TWAIN command located under the Import item of the File menu. If neither exists, check the manual for your third-party software program to see if you can use TWAIN to acquire images from your camera.

If your computer has previously had a scanner, digital camera, or other capturing device installed, it is possible the WIN.INI file needs to be cleared of old TWAIN source entries. Here's how to check for it and what to do about it, if found:

1. Choose Start ⇨ Run, and then, in the Open entry field, type **SYSEDIT**.

2. Click OK.

3. In the System Configuration Editor window, click C:\WINDOWS\WIN.INI to bring that file to the front.

4. On the menu bar of the System Configuration Editor, choose Search ⇨ Find.

5. In the Find window, type **twain**.

6. Click Next.

7. If found, the [TWAIN] section, in brackets, will be highlighted. In this section, check for a line that begins with "Default Source=".

8. If found, remark the line to prevent its execution. Place the cursor in front of the "Default Source=" line, and type a semi-colon (;) at the beginning of the line, as follows:

   ```
   [Twain]
   ;Default Source=C:\Deskscan\dsii.ds
   ```

9. On the System Configuration Editor menu bar choose File ⇨ Save.

10. Close the System Configuration Editor.

11. Reboot your computer and try acquiring the image again.

If TWAIN errors persist, try removing all TWAIN files and their associated TWUNK files. Reinstalling the software should resolve the problem. Follow these steps:

1. Click Start ⇨ Find, and then click Files or Folders.

2. In the Find: All Files dialog box, ensure that (C:) is the only text displayed in the Look In entry box. If any folders are listed after (C:), remove them.

3. Ensure that the Include Subfolders box is checked.

4. In the Named entry box, type **TWAIN**, and then click Find Now.

5. If any files are found, then, on the menu bar of the Find: All Files window, choose Edit ⇨ Select All.

6. On the keyboard press Shift+Delete to permanently erase all selected files.

7. Repeat Steps 2 through 6, substituting **TWUNK** in the Named field.

8. Shut down your computer and restart it.

The computer is now ready for the reinstallation of the HP software.

Glossary

A

aperture

A camera feature that controls how much light enters the camera through the shutter, measured in f-stops — the smaller the f-stop number, the more light is admitted.

autofocus

A lens system that automatically focuses before the exposure is made — a delay of a second or so is required before the shutter opens, enabling the camera to gauge the distance to the subject and focus the lens.

automatic flash

A flash system that automatically determines whether an image requires a flash and provides the correct amount of light — a typical feature on most digital cameras.

B

backlighting

A situation where the main source of light is behind the subject.

binary

The language used by computers to store information and communicate with each other. Binary data is composed of the two values 0 (zero) and 1.

bitmap

An uncompressed image format used within the Windows operating system — bitmaps offer excellent image quality, but they require a large amount of space.

bracketing

A trick used by photographers to ensure proper exposure without a meter, or to ensure a more precise exposure when a meter is used. The photographer takes a series of images — one at the estimated or metered exposure, one slightly over, and one slightly under.

byte

A unit of data — together, a group of eight zeros and ones make a byte (it's also equal to a single character's worth of text).

C

camera obscura

Latin for "dark chamber." A device used to trace objects or a complete scene — it uses mirrors to reflect an image onto a sheet of glass. The camera obscura was a predecessor to today's cameras.

CCD

Short for "charge-coupled device." The most common form of photosensitive cells used to convert incoming light into electrical signals in today's digital cameras.

CD-R

Short for "Compact Disc — Recordable." A recordable CD-ROM disc that can store computer data and digital audio. CD-R discs can be recorded once, and cannot be reused for storage as can CD-RW discs.

CD-ROM

Short for "Compact Disc — Read-Only Memory." A CD-ROM is a compact disc recorded for use with a computer.

CD-RW

Short for "Compact Disc — Rewritable." A CD-RW disc can store information like a CD-R disc, but it can be erased and rewritten over and over.

color intensity

A feature found on most inkjet printers that controls the brightness of an image by varying the amount of ink applied to the page — lighter images use less ink, and darker images use more.

continuous shutter

A feature found on more expensive digital cameras that enables you to take several images in quick succession—the images are saved to the memory card after the multiple exposures have been taken.

cropping

Removing a portion of a photograph, enabling you to remove extraneous objects in the background or edges of the shot.

daguerreotype

A photograph on a copper plate with a silver surface. Daguerreotypes were invented by Louis-Jacques-Mandé Daguerre and were the most popular photographic medium from 1839 until the late 1850s.

depth-of-field scale

A device used by photographers to estimate the distance range where objects are in sharp focus.

digital camera

A camera that saves images as digital files rather than exposing a roll of film.

digital zoom

A feature that enlarges the subject within an image to fill more of the frame. Using a digital zoom reduces the resolution of an image.

downloading

The process of transferring your digital images from your camera to your computer (using any one of a number of different types of connections); once an image has been downloaded, it's saved to your hard drive for later use.

exposure

Admitting light into the body of a camera for a specific amount of time—with a digital camera, the light strikes an array of photosensitive receptors, which convert varying levels of light into electrical current.

F

FAQ

Short for "Frequently Asked Questions." A document containing the answers to the most common questions posed on a subject—for example, a FAQ from a technical support group might itemize common problems that people have using the company's products and the solutions to those problems.

filter

A mathematical formula applied to a digital image. Most image editors offer filters that can make dramatic changes in the appearance of a photograph.

FireWire I

EEE-1394. An interface connection that shares most of the features of USB, although it's less common and transfers data much faster.

fish-eye lens

An extremely wide-angle lens that can take in a huge panoramic view, but distorts the edges of the image.

fixed focus

A lens system that doesn't require focusing. Most "point-and-shoot" automatic cameras have a fixed-focus lens.

focal length

The number of millimeters between the surface of the camera lens and the sensor array at the back of the camera. The focal length of your camera determines how large the subject appears in the image—the greater the focal length, the larger the subject appears. Most digital cameras have a focal length between 35 and 37mm.

focus lock

Also called an infinity lock, this camera feature sets your camera to focus to a certain distance (ignoring closer objects, if present).

focusing

Adjusting a camera's lens system to bring the subject into sharp view.

formatting

Completely erasing and resetting a camera's memory card. This is usually done as a quick way to erase a full card that you want to reuse or to attempt to fix a card that can't be recognized by the digital camera.

G

GIF

Short for "Graphics Interchange Format." A compressed image format that's popular on the Web. GIF was the first commonly-used image format, but it's been largely replaced by JPEG.

gigabyte

A unit of data equal to 1,024MB (megabytes).

H

hard drive

Your computer's permanent storage device for your programs and digital photographs — you can both read data from and write data to a hard drive.

high-drain alkaline batteries

Batteries that deliver the long-lasting power required by today's digital cameras.

I

image editor

A program that enables you to edit and modify any digital image. With an image editor, you can add special effects and fix certain composition problems, as well as add new elements to the image.

infrared

An interface design that requires no wires or cables — data is sent from your digital camera to an infrared receiver on your computer laptop, palmtop, or printer, using the same technology as your TV's remote control.

interface

A standard method of connecting a hardware device to your computer. For a digital camera, common interfaces include USB, serial and FireWire.

J

JPEG

Short for "Joint Photographic Experts Group." The most common image format used by digital cameras. JPEGs are also popular on Web pages, and they're used to send images via e-mail. The JPEG format offers a compression scheme that makes image files far smaller than files in other formats.

K

kilobyte

A unit of data equal to 1,024 bytes.

L

LCD screen

A small screen provided on most digital cameras that enables you to view images you've taken — It can also be used as a viewfinder.

M

macro lens

A lens especially made for extreme close-up photography. A macro lens lets you focus on a subject a few inches or less from the lens surface.

manual flash

A flash system that can be set to fully automatic operation, "always on," or "always off" modes for special circumstances, and can provide a preset amount of light. A digital camera with manual flash should also have connectors for an external synchronized flash unit.

manual focus

A lens system that requires the photographer to set the focus by hand.

megabyte

A unit of data equal to 1,024K (kilobytes).

megapixel

The number of pixels per inch that a digital camera can produce in an image — for example, one megapixel is 1,000 pixels per inch.

memory card

The system used to store images by most digital cameras. Unlike your computer's memory card, however, it retains data even without electricity. Three types of memory cards are in use today: CompactFlash, SmartMedia, and Memory Sticks.

memory card reader

An external unit that accepts a memory card and connects directly to your computer, enabling you to download images from the card much more quickly than downloading from the camera.

metering

The process of measuring the available light reflected from the subject to calculate the proper exposure time or aperture.

optical zoom

A feature that alters a camera's focal length, filling more of the frame with the subject.

orientation

The direction that the length of an image (or a printed page) faces — *portrait* (where the length is positioned vertically) or *landscape* (where the length is positioned horizontally).

parallax

A focusing error introduced in a typical optical rangefinder at extremely close range — it's caused by the discrepancy between your optical viewfinder and your camera's lens (which results from the distance between the viewfinder's window and the lens).

PCMCIA

Short for "Personal Computer Memory Card International Association." These devices are often called PC cards. PCMCIA cards are used to connect hardware such as a modem, network, or external disk drive to your laptop or portable computer. It can also be an adapter that enables you to read your CompactFlash memory card directly into your laptop computer.

photo composition

The art of arranging lighting and the elements in a scene (as well as control of focus and exposure) to produce a great photograph.

photo paper

A heavy paper with a glossy finish that's specifically made for printing high-resolution color photographs with an inkjet printer.

pixel

A single dot within a digital photograph — the photograph is made up of thousands of pixels.

plug-in

A third-party software module that you can buy and install into many image editors. A plug-in provides a new filter or effect that you can apply to your images.

RAM

Short for "Random Access Memory." Your computer's RAM holds the data needed by your computer to run your programs. When you turn off your computer, you lose the contents of RAM, so you'll need to save the data you want to keep to your hard drive.

resizing

Changing the dimensions of an image (measured in pixels) to make it larger or smaller.

resolution

In terms of digital cameras, resolution is usually quoted as the dimension of an image measured in pixels. The figure is expressed as the number of pixels measured in rows (left to right) and columns (up and down).

retina

The area at the back of the human eye that converts incoming light into electrical impulses sent to the brain.

rotation

Turning an image — for example, you might use an image editor to rotate an image to change its *orientation* from portrait to landscape.

Rule of Asymmetry

A photo composition rule that calls for objects of different shapes to be included in the frame, often with a sharp contrast between light and dark.

Rule of Thirds

A photo composition rule that divides the frame into nine equal areas; subjects should be aligned along one of the lines, or appear at an intersection.

secure connection

An encrypted connection offered by an online Web store; when information is encrypted, it's much harder for a hacker to intercept your data as it's being transmitted to the Web site.

semi-automatic flash

A flash system that can be set to fully automatic operation but also has "always on" or "always off" modes for special circumstances.

serial port

A port that enables you to connect external devices such as digital cameras and modems to your computer. A serial connection is the slowest method of downloading images from your camera to your computer.

shutter

The device at the front of the camera that opens when you press the shutter release button — it admits a specified amount of light into the body of the camera for a specified amount of time.

shutter speed

The amount of time a camera shutter remains open to admit light.

telephoto

A lens with a longer focal length and a smaller field of view than a standard primary camera lens. A telephoto is useful for enlarging distant subjects.

temperature

In photography, the specific hue of a color (as measured in degrees Kelvin).

thumbnail

A much smaller version of a digital photograph (usually about the size of a postage stamp). The software provided with your digital camera probably uses thumbnails to display the images stored on a memory card.

TIFF

Short for "Tagged Image File Format." An image format popular among Macintosh owners, graphic artists, and the publishing industry.

tripod

A portable, three-legged stand that photographers use to provide a steady base for a camera. (A camera stand with one leg is called a *monopod*.)

TWAIN

Short for "Technology Without An Interesting Name." The standard interface between software applications and image-capturing devices such as scanners.

USB

Short for "Universal Serial Bus." A popular interface for connecting all sorts of external devices — including digital cameras — to most PC and Macintosh computers. A USB device can be plugged in and used without rebooting your computer.

wide-angle lens

A lens with a shorter focal length and a larger field of view than a standard primary camera lens. Wide-angle lenses are great for shooting scenic photographs.

zoom lens

A lens with an adjustable focal length that lets you view a scene with either a narrow or wide field of view, or anywhere in between. Zoom lenses let you zoom in on just a small part of a larger image, yet also let you zoom out to see more of the image, and are handy for a variety of shots when you don't want to carry multiple lens with you.

Index

storing images
  on CD-R discs, 56–59
  on CD-RW discs, 57–59
  with Jaz drives, 60
  with Orb drives, 60
  summary, 60
  with SuperDisk drives, 59–60
  with Zip drives, 59, 60
Sunburst effect, 123
SuperDisk drives. *See also* storing images
  advantage, 59–60
  drawbacks, 60
  using, 59–60

T

telephoto lens. *See also* lenses
  camera threading for, 19
  defined, 72
  field of view, 72
  focal length and, 72
  uses, 72
temperature, color, 66
test pages, 6
Text Entry dialog box (Paint Shop Pro),
    129
textures
  composition and, 84
  natural beauty, 112
thumbnails, viewing, 42
TIFF format. *See also* formats
  applications, 89
  cons, 89
  defined, 89
  for document photos, 93
  image quality, 22
  pros, 89
tripods
  collapsible, 35
  steadiness and, 35
  using, 28

T-shirt transfers. *See also* crafts
  aligning, 127
  applying, 127–128
  cooling, 128
  creating, 12, 126–128
  design, sealing, 127
  fabric preparation, 126
  ironing, 127
  materials for, 126
  paper, 126
  printers for, 126
  printing, 7, 126–127
  test pages, 126
  trimming, 127
  warning, 127
"tunnel" effect, 65

U

Ulead Photo Explorer
  Convert menu item, 43
  converting images with, 43
  Copy command, 43
  displaying, 42
  Explorer pane, 44
  features, 42–43
  folder tree, 42
  Output HTML Thumbnails dialog box,
    44–45
  thumbnail catalog, 44
  thumbnails, 42
  viewing images with, 42
ultimate set controls, 26
underexposure, 67
USB connection
  cables, 36
  connecting, 35–36
  cost, 23
  defined, 23
  ports, 24, 35, 36

hpshopping.com

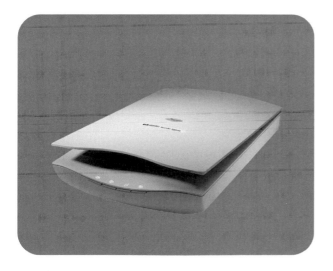